# FROM BELIEF TO BEHAVIOR

## THE POWER OF BELIEF IN BUSINESS

---

## PHIL OLSEN

© 2021 by Philip S. Olsen
All rights reserved. No part of this book may be reproduced in any form or by any electronic or mechanical means, including information storage and retrieval systems, without permission in writing from the author, except by a reviewer who may quote brief passages in a review.

Scripture noted NIV are taken from the HOLY BIBLE: NEW INTERNATIONAL VERSION®. Copyright © 1973, 1978, 1984 by International Bible Society. All rights reserved.

Scriptures noted NASB are taken from the New American Standard Bible®, Copyright © 1960, 1962, 1963, 1968, 1972, 1975, 1977, 1995 by The Lockman Foundation. All rights reserved.

Beyond Sunday, Inc.
5386 Under Way, Sugar Hill, GA 30518

visit our website at www.gobeyondsunday.com

First Beyond Sunday, Inc. printing: March 2021

10 9 8 7 6 5 4 3 2 1

Library of Congress
LCCN: 2021904722

Olsen, Phil 1967-
    From Belief to Behavior: The Power of Belief in Business/ Phil Olsen

ISBN 978-1-7368014-0-6

This book is dedicated to my father,
Philip F. Olsen, whose pursuit of God, life, and
excellence were fundamental to my
discovering the calling of my life.

# Contents

| | |
|---|---:|
| **PREFACE** | 1 |
| **INTRODUCTION** | 5 |
| The Normal Life | 5 |
| The Need for Meaning | 6 |
| The Why Behind My Meaning | 9 |
| Created for Meaning | 10 |
| Discover Your Meaning | 11 |
| **1. CLARIFY YOUR ACTIONS:** | **13** |
| *YOU ARE NOT AN ACTOR* | |
| Achieving the Dream | 13 |
| Distorted Dreams | 14 |
| Unlocking the Code | 19 |
| Your Beliefs May be Picking Your Pocket | 21 |
| Doing v. Valuing | 22 |
| Internal War | 25 |
| The Power of Emotions on the Business Stage | 27 |
| Competition Stress | 29 |
| Conflicting Cultures | 31 |
| Contradicting Internal Beliefs | 33 |

## 2. IGNITE YOUR DREAMS:     37
### *YOUR BELIEF MATTERS*
A Tale of Contrasts      37
Dream Fade      40
If You Believe it, You Can Achieve It      44

## 3. ACQUIRE DIRECTION:     51
### *THE POWER OF A COACH*
Ethical Cheating      51
The Power of a Coach      53
The Necessity of Authority      57
Destructive Authority      60

## 4. ACHIEVE EXTREME ADVANTAGE:     67
### *ESTABLISH YOUR SOURCE OF AUTHORITY*
The Challenge of Being a Sophomore      67
The Challenge of Finding a Trustworthy Authority      70
The Power of a Final Source of Authority      75
Confidence of Biblical Proportions      78

## 5. CONFIRM WHAT IS TRUE:     85
### *THE BIBLE DOES NOT APPLY TO BUSINESS*
Beyond Applying      85
Risky Belief      86
Leadership Principle Breadcrumbs      88
Above Your Paygrade      90
Our Words Tell on Us      92
Counterintuitive      94
My Pleasure      95

| | |
|---|---|
| Universal Effect | 99 |
| The Ripple Effect | 101 |
| Choose | 102 |

## 6. EXPERIENCE EXHILARATION:    109
### *WHEN WHY YOU EXIST DEFINES WHAT YOU DO*

| | |
|---|---|
| Assessing What Inspires You | 111 |
| Three Levels of Internal Purpose | 112 |
| Success | 113 |
| Significance | 114 |
| Soul | 116 |
| The Discrepancy between the Sell and the Experience | 118 |
| From a Job to a Calling | 119 |
| Business Confidence – Finding Your Value | 126 |
| Soul Calling and Value | 127 |

## 7. LEVERAGE YOUR LIFE:    133
### *COMMIT TO ESSENTIAL RISK*

| | |
|---|---|
| The Limits of Success | 135 |
| Success Attachment | 137 |
| An Ultimate Example | 137 |
| Step One - Clarify Your Design, Motives, and Purpose | 143 |
| Step Two - Realize Everything is a Tradeoff | 146 |
| Step Three - Commit to Leverage as the Ultimate Tradeoff | 150 |

## 8. DEFINE YOUR IMPACT: 159
### *CREATING A LEGACY*

The Pull of Legacy 159
The Power of Legacy 162
Life without Leverage 163
Life with Horizontal Leverage 163
Life with Vertical Leverage 165
Degrees of Impact 168
Cost 171
Beyond Crafting a Vision 173
Pause 176

## NOTES 184

# Acknowledgments

I'd like to thank:

My wife, Janan Olsen, whose belief, love, and passion for life have been central to our investing in so many across the years and whose professional skills were used for the final edit of this book.

My father, Philip F. Olsen, who spent untold hours doing the principal editing and gave essential insights throughout the writing process.

The key associates in Beyond Sunday, Inc. who have helped me across the years refine the principles communicated here.

# PREFACE

This book began decades ago as I watched my father and grandfather make impact in the business arena. They were both highly successful – one in the corporate world and the other in the auto industry. They advanced to the top of their field – one as a vice-president with responsibility for multi-billion dollar programs with hundreds of engineers and executives on his teams and the other as an owner of a successful business in an ethically challenged industry.

I watched as their core beliefs defined how they did business and ignited much of their success. While they were not always blatantly overt in promoting their particular beliefs, their beliefs defined fully how they did business and indelibly marked the businesses they led.

The impact of that mindset intrigued me, and while I could not have defined decades prior how it would play out, their example shaped my sense of calling in life. As I moved through college and into graduate school, I began to discover even greater connections between belief and business. Whether religious or secular in their orientation, there was a growing awareness among a number of key business leaders as to the importance and power of belief (or culture) in business.

I have spent decades listening to, learning from, and interacting with numerous leaders from CEOs of international corporations to blue-collar workers who grew to make a difference. Their stories are transformative, and the consistency of the effect of what is shared in this book is proven in their lives over and over again.

Most people have been afraid of bringing their belief into their business, especially if they would define that belief as their faith. The thought is "religion and business don't mix – it is a separation of church and state thing."

I am not intending to convince you regarding some political stance, but this book will challenge you to take another look at how you unite what you believe with what you do. Whether you are an employee, employer, executive, entrepreneur, or just someone who wants to experience their life to the fullest, these pages will clarify why what you believe is everything.

This book is intended for corporate leaders, entrepreneurs, and employees who want to discover the deepest why of their life and the greatest impact for what they do.

While the references and the research that have gone into this book span many disciplines, the concepts in this book are universally biblically based. For some that may be a turnoff. Surprisingly, in my personal interactions and coaching with business leaders, I have rarely found that to be an issue even though many have had significantly different belief systems.

As you will discover, the beliefs we address are far more than a dogma you can quote. They are actually what you believe to be true – your core ways of perceiving the world. And they have defined your life to this point.

If you grasp the connection between your beliefs and your behavior, it will change how you see belief in business and release your ability to change a world.

I look forward to your transformation.


Phil Olsen
Atlanta
February 2, 2021

# FROM BELIEF TO BEHAVIOR

# INTRODUCTION

You are meant for something.

Everything about you being you comes from this essential truth. And to the degree that you grasp this, it creates inside of you a striving to know this meaning, an artesian well of passion. If the realization of your meaning is restricted or tainted, this passion becomes frustration.

You have a life. You get to live. You get to choose. You get to make impact.

What you believe about meaning – especially yours – has everything to do with how you do life and business.

## The Normal Life

How does life normally work?

In education – go to school; get good grades, so you can

go to a good college and get good grades. So you can get a good job and pay for the good college you went to and maybe your kids' college too so they can go to school and get good grades.

In lifestyle – buy a car; get a career; build a house; make a living or should it be called make an existing. Get married; get kids. Buy them good track shoes so they can run the rat race even better.

I love excelling. I love working hard to achieve a goal. But there has to be something more than this.

## The Need for Meaning

Instinctively, we believe things ought to have meaning beyond just existing.

According to Maslow's hierarchy of needs, the pinnacle of life is self-actualization.

Pick your #1 song or movie. It likely focuses on the meaning of life or relationships. Being a hero gives life meaning. Being loved, belonging speak to meaning. Accomplishing is meaning. Visionary dreaming is hoping, believing for meaning.

It is true with wives and husbands – ultimately the greatest thing they desire from their spouse is either to be cherished or respected. For them this is the highest meaning.

We have an innate awareness that life is more than 9 to 5 – that even 9 to 5 should be more than 9 to 5.

How satisfied you are with your present business, relationships, and life arises directly out of how much you have realized the true meaning for what you are doing. This book

## INTRODUCTION

is designed to help you get there.

Steve Jobs achieved a point of fascination in the minds of today's culture. His death cemented him as a cult hero. His approach to business was singular. Roberto Verganti wrote in The Harvard Business Review,

> The reason why institutional management theories have always looked at [Steve Job's] style as an exception is that he was navigating a territory that is often obscure to management: the creation of meaning, both for customers and employees...
>
> "Managing by meaning" is recognizing that people are human: they have rational, cultural, and emotional dimensions, and they appreciate the person who creates a meaning for them to embrace.[1]

Steve Jobs brought unique meaning to products that previously were merely word processors and telephones. The challenge, according to Verganti, is meaning cannot be imitated, so it resists being made into a management process.

But there is a deeper challenge with meaning. If my life is to have meaning, it requires something greater than myself – much in line with Emerson's "hitch your wagon to a star."

> Now that is the wisdom of a man, in every instance of his labor, to hitch his wagon to a star, and see his chore done by the gods themselves. That is the way we are strong, by borrowing the might of the elements. The forces of steam, gravity, galvanism, light, magnets, wind, fire, serve us day

by day and cost us nothing…

And as our handiworks borrow the elements, so all our social and political action leans on principles. To accomplish anything excellent the will must work for catholic and universal ends. A puny creature, walled in on every side, as Daniel wrote,—

"Unless above himself he can

Erect himself, how poor a thing is man!"

but when his will leans on a principle, when he is the vehicle of ideas, he borrows their omnipotence.[2]

Emerson had one idea of where that meaning could come from. You have your own – a belief of what would make your business, your relationships, your life to have prominence, distinction, value.

If we were fully transparent, we are so passionate about achieving meaning we are not even all that concerned about the star we are hitching to. Just make my star go somewhere great. Let me become appreciated as valuable.

Everyone appreciates a good pay check. Yet I would challenge, it isn't only Mother Teresa who would be willing take a reduction in pay, if they knew it meant their meaning would explode. But reducing our income is not how we think meaning happens.

I have found few that would say they are money-hungry. Yet, one of the great draws of money is it feels as if it might be a tool to expand our meaning, our value. It is not only that the rich are valued or esteemed; they have the means of creating value and impact.

This is why perceived value is so powerful. If you can

add perceived value through your business or product, you generate potential for extensive growth.

As I work with business leaders, the primary focus I am looking for is to help them grasp a greater understanding for why they are doing life and business. Simon Sinek refers to it as "start with why."

I have my own reason for what I do.

## The Why Behind My Meaning

In 1982, I was a high school student – dreaming of the conquest of aerospace engineering, leadership management, and experiencing the excitement of the rigors of college education – Rensselaer Polytechnic Institute to be specific. Those were my dreams anyway.

I ran with a group of guys who were educationally, athletically, and career motivated. I listened to and watched them dream. It was exciting – with a pause. I couldn't say exactly what I was seeing or feeling at the time, but there was a hole in the future.

And then my world changed. It all began with this nagging sense that my heretofore confident belief about my future might be off. I might have a different road to go down.

As I watched a number of those I hung around who were on the cusp of success, I realized they were missing a significant component. At a preliminary level, I grasped that faith was not a sideline but an essential fundamental to the productive functioning of business. Success – the visible production of our life – was a great thing, but left to itself it was a ladder that only reached part way up the building.

It was incomplete.

As positive an experience as my faith had been, what I was being drawn to was beyond the kind of ministry I was looking at on the weekend. I would resonate with Frost, "Two roads diverged in a wood and I - I took the one less traveled by, and that has made all the difference."

The last three decades have been spent studying, leading, and coaching people from blue collar to CEO's of international corporations – helping them discover who it is that created them, why He created them, and what it looks like to live that out in the present culture.

Beyond Sunday, the company that I am president of and helped found, is a faith-based organization whose ultimate vision is to see the Kingdom of Christ infused into the workplace and the capabilities of the workplace infused back into the Kingdom. It takes business leaders and inspires them to move from belief to behavior. So you say this is what you believe. What would it look like to live it out in your workplace?

This intersection of faith and function, belief and behavior, gives us a huge advantage in the corporate setting. As clarified in chapter 6, when why you exist is in harmony with what you do, the results are explosive.

## CREATED FOR MEANING

Genesis 2:7 describes how we were created. "The LORD God formed the man from the dust of the ground and breathed into his nostrils the breath of life, and the man became a living being [NIV]." No other created thing included this step. According to Genesis 1:30, every living thing had the "breath of life" in it, but only with human beings did God breathe the breath of life into them.

It was as if God was breathing His creative Spirit into us – and with it the desire for purpose, meaning, impact.

## Discover Your Meaning

What you will read here will give you the means to both clarify the why behind who you are and what you are doing as well as give you actionable steps to leverage the deepest parts of who you are.

It will help you understand how to develop a soul level motivation that will transform your business and life.

I would make the audacious claim that, if your life is fulfilling, it has little to do with how much you make or what you have.

That may not sound audacious. You have heard, "money can't buy me love" – thank you 1964 Beatles. But if you can get beyond the sappy sentimentalism or the apparent pandering to piety and get to the core of what drives us – money does not drive us. It is the desire for the fulfillment and value that money might bring that is the draw.

You want to do something that has meaning. You don't just want to pay bills and get things. Even your love of sports or romance is a desire for vicarious meaning. If you are an entrepreneur, the conquest has attraction because it has the potential for great value and meaning.

And so you should because you were meant for something. You were designed to have meaning.

So come on a journey with me toward what you believe, what you are meant for, and why that is determining how you do life and business. Discover how you can change what you and others believe and how this will renovate your world.

# 1

# Clarify Your Actions:
## You Are Not an Actor

### Achieving the Dream

Ken grew up in the inconsequential mid-western town of Tyrone, Missouri. Today it's over 50 miles to the nearest interstate. Even more telling is the true American litmus test of importance... it's over 10 miles to the nearest Walmart in the big town of Houston, MO – population 2,093.

In 1942, when Ken was born, Tyrone was far more remote. Growing up there, he understood poverty. His dad was a lay minister and worked as a salesman while attempting to run a business. Ken's early childhood was upended when his dad's feed store went under. His family was forced to move in with relatives on a farm. It wasn't until Kenneth was 11 that he lived in a house with plumbing.

Both the poverty and his dad being a lay minister marked Ken's life and formed his character. He was determined to never be poor, and he grew up being infused with values founded on deeply held ethical beliefs.

Ken was a good student, but academic scholarships weren't enough to pay the full cost of attending the University of Missouri, so he took out loans, worked painting houses, and did whatever it took to both pay for school and get his education. When he discovered economics in a beginning class on the subject, he was hooked. His professor Pinkney Walker persuaded him to solidify the business benefit of Ken's new major by earning his master's degree.

His life moved quickly. After graduation, Ken went from Humble Oil, soon to be Exxon, worked on his doctorate, and in 1968 enlisted in the Navy. Walker, Ken's professor and mentor, continued to support his new protégé by getting Ken a navy procurement position in Washington, D.C. Following his enlistment, Ken moonlighted teaching night school at George Washington University while he finished his PhD – during which time he married his college sweetheart, Judith Ayers.

By 34, he was already the corporate president of Florida Gas. He became a role model for chief executives and, while highly successful, was best known for just being a nice man. He received numerous leadership awards, was inducted into the Business Hall of Fame, and received the Horatio Alger Award for Distinguished Americans.

## Distorted Dreams

Yet in 1980, a discrepancy started to surface between his

external persona as contrasted to his true internal beliefs. No one seemed to notice, but Ken asked for a separation from his wife in order to pursue an affair with his secretary. Two years later, his divorce was finalized and he married his lover, Linda.

Ken went through numerous career advancements until at 43 he was appointed CEO of a large and quickly growing energy corporation, initially named HNG/InterNorth. He organized massive change and at 44 was given $731,000 in cash compensation.

While there is nothing immoral about being wealthy, Ken's business and personal lifestyles were lavish by most anyone's standards. His corporation had a fleet of jets that flew Ken and his family wherever they wanted to go and he owned over 20 houses and estates.

Ken led the company through apparent massive growth rising at lightning speed up the ranks of the Fortune 500.

> One of [the company's] weirdest moments occurred in 1998 when [Ken] and other corporate bigwigs led Wall Street analysts through the trading floor of the… Energy Services divisions, which was abuzz with employees cutting deals and making trades. It was impressive; it was also fake. The floor had previously been vacant and had been filled with employees told to look as though they were doing something simply to impress the visitors. This episode suggested that [Ken] was at ease with [his company's] duplicitous practices.[1]

You may or may not know Ken Lay by name, but you

surely have heard of his company – Enron. Ken had created what appeared to be an amazing company. In 1996 its competitors voted Enron as the most innovative company in the U.S. as revealed in Fortune magazine, putting them ahead of such high-tech giants as Intel and Microsoft.[2] In 2000, Fortune magazine ranked them as #5 on "America's Most Admired Companies," #1 for "Innovativeness," and #2 for "Getting & Keeping Talent."[3]

In his book, *Normal Organizational Wrongdoing*, ethics philosopher Donald Palmer said:

> Enron's chairman, Ken Lay, considered himself a value-based leader and spoke often about the importance of considering moral issues when making business decisions (cf. Novak 1996). ... By all accounts he was an intensely religious man, a Baptist, who attended church regularly and taught Sunday school.

The referenced Michael Novak book, *Business As a Calling*, quotes Ken's passion as,

> I was, and am, a strong believer that one of the most satisfying things in life is to create a highly moral and ethical environment in which every individual is allowed and encouraged to realize their God-given potential.[4]

Nevertheless,

> In the early 2000s Ken fell from admired leader to despised failure: he looted billions of dollars for the sake of self-aggrandizement and self-indulgence, bringing about

catastrophe for tens of thousands of victims and misery for millions more.[5]

When Enron went bankrupt, 21,000 people lost their jobs, their pensions, and for many their life savings – all of which were tied up in Enron and Enron stock.

A May 25, 2006 ABC News report summed up the results of the investigation into Enron:

> Former Enron executives Ken Lay and Jeffrey Skilling have been found guilty of fraud and conspiracy.
>
> Lay, 64, was convicted on all six counts against him, including conspiracy to commit securities and wire fraud. He faces a maximum of 45 years in prison. Lay also faces 120 years in prison in a separate case.
>
> "I firmly believe I'm innocent of the charges against me." Lay said following the hearing. "We believe that God in fact is in control and indeed he does work all things for good for those who love the Lord."
>
> In a separate, nonjury bank fraud trial related to Lay's personal banking, U.S. District Judge Sim Lake found the Enron founder guilty of bank fraud and making false statements to banks. Lake had withheld his verdict in the Lay bank fraud case until the Lay-Skilling jury announced its verdict. Lay faces up to 120 years in prison in that case.[6]

A month and a half later, Ken died of a heart attack while vacationing in Colorado.

Ironically, its 2000 annual report lists these as Enron's values:

*Communication:* We have an obligation to communicate. Here, we take the time to talk with one another… and to listen. We believe that information is meant to move and that information moves people.

*Respect:* We treat others as we would like to be treated ourselves. We do not tolerate abusive or disrespectful treatment.

*Integrity:* We work with customers and prospects openly, honestly and sincerely. When we say we will do something, we will do it; when we say we cannot or will not do something, then we won't do it.

*Excellence:* We are satisfied with nothing less than the very best in everything we do. We will continue to raise the bar for everyone. The great fun here will be for all of us to discover just how good we can really be.

After the Enron, WorldCom, and other scandals, Congress did an investigation on "Oath Taking, Truth Telling, and Remedies in the Business World." They invited Truett Cathy, founder of Chick-fil-A, to speak to them.

After agreeing to appear before you today, I had to ask myself, "What is the meaning of 'business ethics'?" I concluded that there is really no such thing as business ethics. There is only personal ethics. I believe no amount of business school training or work experience can teach what is ultimately a matter of personal character. Businesses are not dishonest or selfish, people are. Thus, a business, successful or not, is merely a reflection of the character of its leadership.

During this same congressional hearing, Dr. Murphy Smith, professor of accounting at Texas A&M University clarified,

> The purpose of ethics in business is to direct business men and women to abide by a code of conduct that facilitates, if not encourages, public confidence in their products and services… When societal values are deteriorating, maintaining high ethical standards in accounting and business grows increasingly difficult.[7]

## Unlocking the Code

How does someone go from admired to despised? How does a nice guy bilk people out of billions? Was it a charade from the beginning? Was all of this a big scam from early on? Was Lay a good guy who succumbed to the influence of Skilling?

Why do people do what they do? I've interviewed a man who fought for Hitler and another who came to the aid of Martin Luther King, Jr., even though he was Caucasian. The latter negotiated with the leadership in Selma, AL convincing them to give the marchers the necessary support to host and sustain their march.

Yet both these individuals seemed fully convinced.

If you could unlock the internal code behind our actions, what would you find? That's what this book, *From Belief to Behavior*, unlocks.

The powerful key you will discover is that every conscious action you take results from your true personal values. Actions are not simple choices. They are value statements.

You are not an actor. You are a valuer. I don't mean you shouldn't be an actor. You aren't one. Even con artists are fundamentally valuers. Their values drive their desire to put on an act. In fact, most people are incapable of being con artists – not because they lack the skill but because their values are not sufficiently distorted.

In addition, the values that you have are not will-o'-the-wisps arising out of the mist. Your values did not just happen. They come from what you believe to be true. You believe something to be true, and it is that belief that inspires you to have the values you do. Your actions simply reflect your values.

But that is not the end of the story. The reality is that behind every belief is what sociologists call a worldview. We're talking about something far deeper than just *how* you view the world. The real essence of the matter is *why* you view the world the way you do.

What we are getting at is the "soul" level of who you truly are.

In actuality, the effect of belief on behavior is constantly at work in your life. It is why businesses run the way they do – and even why teenagers act the way they do.

The movement of worldview to belief to behavior defines you – as well as everything around you.

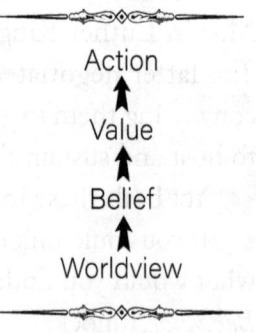

If you can discover and harness this movement, you can change your world.

## Your Beliefs May be Picking Your Pocket

Even if you have momentarily been persuaded that belief is fundamental to actions, most people still inherently assume they are actors – people whose lives are primarily determined by their actions or physical choices.

In support of Einstein's theory of relativity, he reportedly said that insanity is doing the same thing over and over again while expecting different results. The challenge is much of life feels essentially the same, day in and day out. Over time, the repetitive patterns of life can be unsettling. It may be part of the reason you picked up this book.

Within some there builds a burning desire to improve and develop – to actually make changes in their life and business. They take Einstein's or some similar challenge and begin analyzing their actions. It would seem that change is a simple process of deciding to act differently.

There is clear value and often immediate impact to getting an accurate picture of actions, habits, and tendencies. As you become increasingly aware of your actions, you may begin to think you really do understand who you are and what you need to change. If you are purposefully choosing your actions – planning your work and working your plan – you might believe you have your life under control.

This is what I call "the deception of paying attention."

Apollo Robins is a master pickpocket. In describing how he will rip you off, he confides that "One of the most common things I steal is watches." To demonstrate his technique, he tells people "In three minutes I'm going to be wearing your watch. Try to catch me if you can."

He starts by shaking your hand. Then he takes one small

step at a time – even as you believe you are in control of the situation. Your perception of your immediate surroundings is intensified. Obviously, this is particularly true once he has warned you of his objective.

Apollo explains, "I can open their watch in a handshake. The watch is virtually loose but they can't feel it because I hold it closed with three fingers. With their hand gripping mine, they have control. And that's the big thing – that they have the illusion they have control."

He continues, "They have never let go of my hand. It would seem that I would have had to have a third hand to steal the watch, and they think they are in control." And yet he ends up wearing their watch.

Apollo's technique is tied to inciting and following the meanderings of your attention. He says there is a dark space around the spotlight of your attention which "is where I dance. I play in the dark around where your attention moves." [8]

We all tend to have the illusion that our actions simply reflect the choices we make. So we are focused on our actions. We may even be confident of our vigilance in doing so.

Yet in the meantime, your beliefs are stealing you blind. They are "playing in the dark around where your attention moves." These values or underlying beliefs are always with you – and they inevitably determine your actions. But we rarely are aware of the connection.

## Doing v. Valuing

Have you ever found yourself frustrated because you can't get the people under you, around you or over you to take the actions you feel they should? No matter how clearly you define the preferred future, they repeat the same practices. Do you understand the same frustration in inspiring your own change? These may very well be the most common dilemmas faced by every person who aspires to leadership.

The president of one organization told me that after initial significant growth, they had entered a protracted period of stagnation. In analyzing their organization, I observed various external threats and obstacles. But these were not the real problem.

Central to their struggles were staffing and management issues – specifically one particular area. They originally had filled the essential leadership positions from within. But once the need for leadership outstripped the available talent pool, they found it necessary to open up their hiring from outside the organization.

The competence of the new hires was invigorating. But the cost of this new talent was the injection of different values.

Unfortunately, all they saw was the subsequent conflicting actions that lead to leadership turnover and internal conflict. They didn't understand that their problem was that they had replaced insufficient leadership ability with incompatible leadership values.

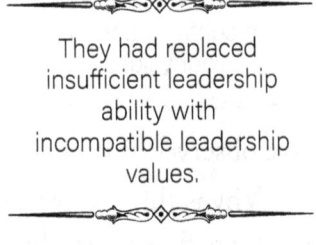
They had replaced insufficient leadership ability with incompatible leadership values.

At the root of their conflicting actions were conflicting values.

No matter what your competency, you cannot consistently act in contradiction to your values.

This is true even if you suspect your values are distorted or unproductive. Until you experience a change in what you value, you cannot achieve permanent change in your actions.

Our failure to change actions often stems from attempting to adjust behavior while understanding little of the values which led to that behavior. This reality exists whether it is a personal attempt to improve or when someone in leadership is trying to guide the behavior of employees.

We tend to focus on actions because they are the most obvious culprits. Because we only have so much attention to give, and actions seem to be the source of our troubles, we focus on behavior.

Self-help teaching can be invigorating when the approach is communicated effectively. Often people are inspired by the ideas which are presented.

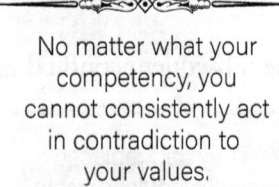
No matter what your competency, you cannot consistently act in contradiction to your values.

Yet survey after survey shows that within a relatively short period, most people are back to their old routines, no matter how much less productive they actually are. You may have observed this phenomenon yourself. I know I have.

Why is this the case? Because the previously accepted beliefs are fundamentally still in place. Your true underlying values have usurped or distorted what you were impressed with in that conference, book, message, or pep talk.

As a result, the most common outcome is frustration and disillusionment. You may have been enamored by the potential reflected in the recent inspirational presentation, but you still are irritatingly unmoved in your eventual actions.

## Internal War

If you have a Christian background, you may have felt as if the church or the Bible was giving you a bunch of laws merely to make you feel guilty. That uncomfortable feeling often comes as you are confronted with the rules but question the benefit. You may accept they have benefit like cauliflower or brussel sprouts but not like a sudden business success or an amazing new romantic relationship. It is the benefit of following through on a "got to" requirement but not the joy of experiencing a "get to" opportunity.

If you own a business, your employees will tend to feel the same way about many of your top down requirements. They chose to work for you because it looked like a good idea. Your business was successful. Your benefits were excellent. Even more, the opportunities seemed exciting. But actually working for you loses a little of the luster.

There is an inherent contradiction inside of us where we hold competing values and beliefs in suspension. A brilliantly revealing description of this is found biblically in the Book of Romans. Paul describes a frustrating, even infuriating, pattern of failure created by an internal conflict. On the one hand he believed fully that what God had described in the law was good, but on the other he kept finding himself repeating the failed patterns of the past. This is how he described it. "I do not understand what I do. For what I want to do I do not do, but what I hate I do." [Romans 7:15 NIV] Welcome to two weeks after an inspiring conference!

In fact, he even calls it a war. "For in my inner being I delight in God's law; but I see another law at work in me, waging war against the law of my mind and making me a prisoner of the law of sin at work within me." [Romans 7:22, 23 NIV]

Paul finishes by saying the issue is our natural patterns and beliefs are in contradiction to what the law describes as quality and necessary. To further exacerbate the problem we are far more convinced of our ability to change our actions than reality gives us the right to be. Paul is fully convinced that he really does want to live differently which makes his repetition of stupid even more internally irritating. His only hope is that the Spirit of God would internally change what he thinks, what he believes [cf. Romans 8:3, 4; 12:1, 2]

This is a powerful truth that is impactful no matter what you declare you believe. We will describe later why we believe there is such significant benefit in placing high ultimate value and trust in what is found in the Bible – why it is especially powerful in business.

Paul was clarifying that what is internal within you makes its way to the outside of you. In poker it is called a "tell."

Back to Apollo Robbins as he does a street trick. His question to those passing by is can you lie well? Can you keep a straight face, a poker face? He gives them a cup with one die in it, tells them to shake the cup, look at the die inside, and then respond to his questions with only one answer – "No."

He proceeds to ask them one-by-one whether it was a 1, 2, 3...6. The first guy only makes it to 2 and Apollo already knows the number. Try as hard as you may to avoid it, what is believed, what is valued, ultimately gets out into action.[9] You can't even say the word "no" without what you believe revealing itself.

This is true about every reality that involves people – individuals, businesses, families, sports teams. Any person, any organization is a reflection of its beliefs. This would be more obvious if I consistently chose one value over another. But we are consistently inconsistent. Today I may choose one way, tomorrow another. Today I get the salad. Tomorrow the Dulce de Leche Caramel Cheesecake. Have my beliefs, my values, changed that fast?

> Try as hard as you may to avoid it, what is believed, what is valued, ultimately gets out into action.

The challenge is we are a complex amalgamate of competing values and beliefs. If it were not for our contradictory actions, we may never be the wiser. The heart is a very advanced internal deceiver. In fact, it has convinced most of us that it has nothing to do with business.

## The Power of Emotions on the Business Stage

We all know in order to make good decisions, you have to keep your emotions out of them. Chris Voss was the lead international kidnapping negotiator among ten thousand FBI agents. His experience involved more than two decades in the FBI. In his book, *Never Split the Difference – Negotiating as if Your Life Depended on It*, Voss describes how he used these same approaches to dominate in a Harvard Law School's Winter Negotiation Course. He characterized his approach simply as "emotionally attuned negotiating techniques."

He cut his teeth negotiating with kidnappers while people's lives hung in the balance, but he was pleasantly amazed at how radically effective the same concepts were in the business negotiations of Harvard Law School. As Voss describes it, "we are always… acting and reacting first and foremost from our deeply held but mostly invisible and inchoate fears, needs, perceptions, and desires."[10]

The reality – our emotions, which follow our values and beliefs, are a part of everything we do. We may attempt to keep them in check, but they ultimately play a central role. If you assume you can play an acting role and manhandle your actions without addressing your beliefs, you have bought into your own heart's deception.

Emotions are the continually resident barometers of what is true about our values and beliefs and how they relate to our actions and the world around us. While wholly emotionally guided decisions are equivalent to the tail wagging the dog, to ignore emotions is equivalent to the dog running blind. Voss' challenge is that all decisions are ultimately emotional. He describes we have two systems at work in our brains. The first is "fast, instinctive, and emotional." The second is "slow, deliberate, and logical." Of these, the first is "far more influential. In fact, it guides and steers our rational thoughts." He goes on to describe that we are "driven by two primal urges: the need to feel safe and secure, and the need to feel in control."[11]

Each of these are at play in the way we do business. So it should not be surprising when the great concepts of the conference or the well-researched ideas of corporate consultants are relegated to a prominent place on the shelf alongside all of our other trophies and nonfunctioning trinkets of life and business. Our beliefs have been stirred but unaltered. So our actions are periodically affected at best.

It is these periodically changing actions that can be the most frustrating. We get momentary glimpses of what could be only to fall back into what has always been. This may be the common lot but it need not be the only lot of life. As agonizing as they may be, your apparent failure may in the end be your savior. Your actions are the symptoms of the reality of what is you. If you were by some means successful in eliminating or disguising your symptoms, it would only prove to cause you to forget reality or assume that your true values and beliefs no longer exist.

As a business friend of mine, Bob Lamp'l, says, "Failure is not an option. It is just a nagging possibility that keeps you focused."

## COMPETITION STRESS

If your conflicting actions weren't evidence enough of your conflicting beliefs, there is a final nail in your acting coffin. You were not created to be an actor, and you weren't created to live with competing values and beliefs remaining internally resident. If your actions don't consistently align with your declared values and beliefs, we have a word for what results – stress! When you internally get out of alignment, the number one symptom you experience is stress.

If changing your actions were the sum of the challenge, stress would not so consistently raise its ugly head. When you think of the competing requirements of your life, you begin to get an external picture of what often is going on internally.

If you consider what you do as a career as valuable, if you consider investment in your family as a priority, if you understand the necessity of creating margin in your life for relaxation, and if you are spiritually attuned to pursue the presence of God – you have just named four significant and apparently competing values. The competition is primarily visible in regard to time and energy.

> When you internally get out of alignment, the number one symptom you experience is stress.

Aside from the area of relaxation, while some have indicated that "showing up" is 50% of the battle, no one is satisfied with you merely showing up. In fact, even if you are on vacation, if you show up at the office, there is an immediate expectation by those working that you should be available. One of my offices is in my home. If my family is home and I am writing in my office during the regular workday, in many ways in their mind I'm still fair game. Just being home does not mean anything if I'm inaccessible.

Because true multitasking is a myth and we don't have omnipresence down, competing expectations create a tug-of-war tension. These are visible, observable, tangible. However, what you don't see and are often unaware of is a far more insidious competitive stress in your life – belief competition. And it comes in at least two forms.

## Conflicting Cultures

The first is conflicting cultures – that is, cultures that are in conflict with your held beliefs. I indicated earlier that you cannot consistently act in contradiction to your values. But what if the culture you are acting in is bringing pressure to do so? Peer pressure is a phrase that conjures up thoughts of our middle and high school years. But there is as much if not more peer pressure in the workplace as there was in your secondary education.

If you have a high sense of moral value but your job metrics encourage less than full honesty in advertising, acquiescing to the culture defined by that standard will create stress. If you value decisive thinking and actions, but your corporate structure is thorough to the point of being painstakingly meticulous, following the cultural norms will be stressful.

Harkening back to Paul and his letter to the Romans, if your own values promote one approach to life but you in momentary decisions act contrary to these, the result is internal war – high emotional and spiritual conflict. Whether you describe it as stress, guilt, anxiety, regret, confusion, frustration, depression – to put it mildly, it is not a good thing. Your internal competition is like two horses pulling in competition instead of in sync. Like the screech of violins a quarter step out of tune with each other.

The challenge here is not merely to understand that this first type of competition exists, it is to respond to the challenge with movement, transformation, solutions. Dealing with this conflict is a key area we will address in later chapters. But understand this at the outset. What initially appears like an impossible conflict or a foregone conclusion as to how you must respond may be far from it. Most assume that the culture or the setting determines their available choices. Our internal default assumption is our present reality is an unavoidable consequence of the way things are – things like contradicting values, actions driven by the business culture, and personal habitual responses.

A couple of months ago a lady was attempting to cross three lanes of traffic to enter a shopping mall parking lot. In the heavy Atlanta traffic, she took her chances and gunned the accelerator to cross the lanes with one error – she didn't see my car and drove both of our cars into the parking lot. Apparently she thought I needed to go shopping. My car was totalled; but thankfully, I was unaffected, and she had insurance.

My neighbor also had to deal with an insurance company recently. He asked how my process went. I said, fine. I ended up getting twice what their insurance company originally offered me. He looked at me quizzically. He didn't realize you had an option to refuse – that the insurance company was making an offer not a determination. While the option to refuse the insurance company's initial offer may be a fairly common understanding, most have my neighbor's understanding when it comes to the contradictory challenges that the business environment or our own previous tendencies create.

You have options. The stress and other negative emotions resulting from belief discord are not a life requirement. They are not a foregone conclusion. And jettisoning your present difficult situation is not the only solution. Job transitions are at times a necessity, but they are far less of a necessity than you might assume. There are rarely two people that think exactly alike. Neither are there companies and employees that have the same values and belief systems at every level. Understanding that, it is still true that competition stress is not a regular necessity. We will clarify how to deal with and influence competing values and beliefs in your business culture.

You have options.

## Contradicting Internal Beliefs

The second source of competition stress is internally contradicting beliefs. The first source is when external actions or environments run contrary to your internal beliefs. The second is when the contradiction is fully internal. Few are aware of the degree of competing values and beliefs resident within. Because of that, all of those negative psychological, physiological, and spiritual emotions we referred to previously are actually godsends.

When it comes to pain, our natural response is to figure out how to get rid of it and get rid of it quickly. But stress and its related cousins are beautiful clarifiers of the state of our internal belief systems. They are the "idiot lights" on the dashboard of our life. When they light up, it indicates an internal challenge.

If your life were primarily comprised of individual decisions, these warning indicators would have limited meaning or benefit. But you are a valuer not an actor. So the internal gauges of your life are regularly measuring the cohesiveness of your values more than the cohesiveness of your actions. Salad yesterday and cheesecake today creates no visceral reaction unless the choices are connected to internal beliefs.

Because your actions are value based they have value. Your motives create motivation. The converse is also true. Belief conflict undermines preceived value. Watch the response of customers or voters to hypocrisy – even if the hypocrisy has no direct connection to the product. Likewise, value conflict demotivates. Internal business value or culture conflict undermines morale in a moment.

Achieving consistent and productive actions is highly beneficial, but unless they actively reflect consistent and commensurate values and beliefs they are empty and most likely short lived.

# BELIEF TRANSFORMATION

## CHAPTER 1
Calibrate your beliefs:

- Every action has at its source something you value.

- Every value comes from what you believe to be true.

- Every belief arises out of your worldview.

- This movement from worldview to action is defining you.

- If you can clarify and harness this movement in your life, you can change your world.

- Our human tendency is to ignore our deepest beliefs and focus only on our actions.

- No matter what your competency, you cannot consistently act in contradiction to your values.

- Until you change what you value, you cannot achieve permanent change in your actions.

- The heart is a very advanced internal deceiver. It convinces most people that soul beliefs and emotions have nothing to do with business.

- The problem of internally competing values and beliefs exacerbates the challenge of changing.

- The number one symptom that indicates you have competing or misaligned values is stress.

- There are two primary sources of belief conflict or "competition stress" – external and internal.

- External conflict comes to a head when your internal values conflict with those of the culture around you.

- Internal conflict becomes apparent when what I think I believe doesn't match the way I act.

What have I become aware of?

What areas do I need to address?

What actions or habits need to change for me to achieve what I'm designed and passionate for?

If my present actions and habits are defining my true values and beliefs, what are those values and beliefs?

# 2

# IGNITE YOUR DREAMS
## YOUR BELIEF MATTERS

### A TALE OF CONTRASTS

In the early 1800's the final frontier was not space. It was the continent of Africa. On December 8, 1840 a 27-year-old Brit from the village of Blantyre set out on a voyage for Africa. Single and with little funding, he was stepping into a continent that was almost impossible to traverse. At that time it was known as the "Dark Continent" and the "White Man's Graveyard."

He landed at the Cape and began his trek up into the center of Africa on his own. He primarily came as a missionary – but he contrasted himself with the "dumpy sort of person with a Bible under his arms." He felt he was "serving Christ when shooting a buffalo for my men, or taking an astronomical observation," even though "some will consider it not sufficiently, or even at all, missionary."

His mission was basically impossible. It was called the "Dark Continent" because so little was known about it. It was the "White Man's Graveyard" because so many had died trying to discover it.

Just 25 years earlier several incredibly well-funded, professionally staffed, and highly touted expeditions had set out and failed miserably. In 1816, naval expedition commander, James H. Tuckey, along with University of Copenhagen trained botanist, Christen Smith, as well as a zoologist, a geologist, a marine biologist, and a gardener from Kew had set out to explore Africa but had failed in their endeavor.

Another fruitless expedition followed soon thereafter. It included – in addition to their British team – "69 Royal African Corps troops, 32 African civilians, 200 pack animals, several field cannon, various other weapons, a plentiful supply of gifts for local rulers, and the standard necessities for such a large force."[1] The list goes on and on of attempts with universal failure.

So what went wrong? According to one summary of James Tuckey's writings,[2] they "encountered suspicion and resistance from Africans whose cooperation it required." The Africans "suspected the expedition's aim was to shut down the slave trade" even though Tuckey gave his "assurances of not coming to prevent the slave trade, or to make war." Aside from that, key people deserted, and "the fatal blow came as a result of the region's dreaded disease environment… one by one, its members fell ill."[3]

Oddly enough, what stopped these expeditions was child's play in comparison to what the 27-year-old Brit had to endure – for he faced almost endless challenges.

The fatal cattle-sickness fell like a plague upon the oxen pulling his wagon and killed them all. He was attacked by a lion that "crunched the bones of his arm." His medicine chest was plundered, and his portable boat was lost. He was twice thrown from his ox, once on his head and once in the middle of a ford. He had thirty-one attacks of fever and had to be his own doctor and nurse.

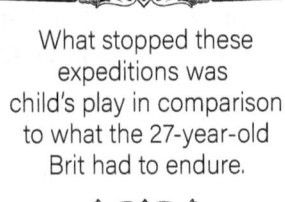

What stopped these expeditions was child's play in comparison to what the 27-year-old Brit had to endure.

The Makololo that he paid to help him were cowards and often wanted to go back. Many deserted him. Multiple times his entire crew either died from illness or quit the expedition. When sending for supplies, it was rare that they got through. Most of the time they were pillaged and sold by the very people paid to bring them.

In addition, it was not only suspected that he was opposed to the slave trade, he actually was pivotal in shutting it down. Besides that, it wasn't until his 1856 return to England that he received sufficient support. Prior to that, for more than a decade and a half, he basically self-funded his own trips.

This young Brit was David Livingstone.

In the words of the historian Vautier Golding:

> David Livingstone began life in a workman's cottage, without knowledge or skill, and without money to obtain them. Yet, when he died, the world was so full of praise and wonder at his work that his body was brought from Africa to rest in Westminster Abbey among the graves of his country's greatest men. He had grown to be a great

pioneer, an explorer, a scientist, a doctor, a missionary, a freer of slaves.[4]

What was the difference between the highly funded and exceptionally staffed British expeditions and the impossibly underfunded and ill-staffed Livingstone? One thing – belief. Golding went on:

> Defeated and disappointed as he was, Livingstone would not give in, for he knew that he was working in God's cause. He also firmly believed that, if he could only make his countrymen really understand the wicked cruelty and waste in Africa, they would come to the rescue."
>
> It is a brave thing to die for one's fellow-men; it is also brave, and often far harder, to live for them. Livingstone did both. Indeed, the humble Blantyre mill-boy had done the noblest and highest thing that man can do; he had given his whole life to help God's less happy creatures. And this he had done, not for money nor for fame, but out of love for God and man."[5]

## Dream Fade

One of the primary causes of businesses failing is a lack of money; however, you cannot fund yourself beyond your belief. Belief matters.

The Torrance® Tests of Creative Thinking were designed to test the creative or divergent thinking of children between kindergarten and 12th grade. With numerous adaptations to the original test, over a quarter of a million children have been evaluated since 1966.

What has been continuously apparent is creativity tends to decrease as education increases. For example, there were marked declines between kindergarten and 3rd grade, as well as after 6th grade.

The same tendency has been observed regarding idealism and dreams. As people progress through adulthood, life experience has a way of sucking the vibrancy from their once lofty goals. For those who remain undaunted by the obstacles, the challenge becomes how to maintain creativity and dreams in the face of a tidal wave of inertia.

Whether it is establishing a new business, reinvigorating an old one, or more personally doing the same thing with regard to relationships, how do I achieve my goals? For that matter, what is worthy of being my goal? Is it worth the struggle and potential disappointment to pour my heart into my goals?

Having had the honor to invest in the lives of young people, one of the things that makes me smile is the immediate juxtaposition of belief and uncertainty that lives within many youth. If they are inspired to engage you, they tend to be very vocal in their beliefs. They are frustrated by others telling them what they are to think and do – yet they are equally as dogmatic in telling you what they believe you ought to think and do. Even so, a short time later their beliefs may have swung wildly in another direction.

I smile as I recognize how little concern they have for the change. Their internal dogmatism is not swayed for a moment. Past beliefs are merely chalked up to the ignorance of "when they were little" – a phrase that my dad use to respond to with, "When was that, last week?"

As divergent and impressionable as their beliefs are, what is equally amazing is the power of their beliefs. Clearly, anyone who continues to develop in life becomes more capable the older they get. Yet some of the most impactful businesses of our day have been started by mere novices who had no right to be so bold.

A couple of the more widely well-known were Steve Jobs and Steve Wozniak. They started Apple when Jobs was just 21. Another is Mark Zuckerberg. Facebook made him a billionaire by the time he was 25.

But there are numerous others as well. David Karp started Tumblr when he was 20 and was worth $22 million by the time he was 23. Sergey Brin & Larry Page started Google at 25. And Matt Mullenweg just turned 19 when he started WordPress from the b2 codebase. WordPress now powers 20% of the world's websites. And that is just scratching the surface.

The same phenomenon is exemplified in other businesses. Philip Knight was still 25 when he first partnered with Bill Bowerman to form Blue Ribbon Sports, later named Nike. Sandra Lerner and Leonard Bosack were 29 and 32 respectively when they formed Cisco. And Earling Persson was 30 when he started H&M, the apparel retailer with over 100,000 employees and an estimated net worth of $40 billion.

This is not just a phenomenon of the present era. The Egyptian pharaoh King Tutankhamun died at 19. Mary Shelley wrote *Frankenstein* when she was 19. Joan of Arc did all of her exploits before she was 20.

For many of these, their youthfulness is an assurance that they could not have had enough experience to legitimize the extent of their success. Granted, there is the enthusiastic energy of youth. But, if you are an entrepreneur, while there is nothing like the impact of relentless energy, energy by itself doesn't guarantee success.

As David Livingstone demonstrated, everyone who strives for significance hits brick walls, unforeseen failures, and is blindsided by experiences and relational hits that they didn't see coming – and which hurt more than they could have imagined. Energy is helpful, but after a few shots to the solar plexus if the only thing you have is energy, you will be face down on the mat without any remaining incentive to get up.

There is a belief beyond belief that ultimately defines your future. It is woven into the economy of existence. It is not mere pep rally fodder. Even though "belief beyond belief" can be used to peddle the latest pabulum, the reason it is so easy to promote is beliefs actually do have a great deal of power.

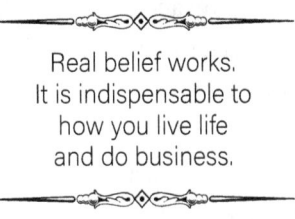

Real belief works. It is indispensable to how you live life and do business.

While this book will help you understand much about why it matters, how to harness it, and its source – there is a fundamental reality to belief that is beyond quantifying. To put it simplistically, real belief works. It is indispensable to how you live life and do business.

## If You Believe it, You Can Achieve It

Now for a little honesty in advertising – the phrase "If you believe it, you can achieve it" drives me crazy. It totally sounds like snake oil, and the only thing I can think of when I hear it is the leader of a bunch of huckster used car salesmen in a sales meeting. The phrase comes across as without any concern for real integrity with regard to truth.

Clearly there are a number of things that are impossible no matter what you believe, like wanting to play professional basketball if you are short - unless your name is Spud Web (5' 6"), Isaiah Thomas (5'9"), or Muggsy Bogues (5'3"). And it's foolish to believe that you can compose great works of music after you have gone deaf – unless your name is Beethoven, Ignaz Hozbauer, Bedrich Smetana, or Vaughan Williams.

Can you feel the confusion? On the one hand, I instinctively react against the oversell of an excited, emotionally-driven reliance on belief. On the other hand, I've got to recognize that even apparently ridiculous belief sometimes has had dramatic success.

How accurate or unlimited is the phrase "If you believe it, you can achieve it?" We will look deeper into that. But suffice it to say, your belief is one of the greatest untapped powers you have. And while I might struggle with the phrase, it has a number of disturbingly regular corroborating evidences.

Biblically speaking, faith is the one heart-action that you can do that moves God. As important as obedience is to God, the one thing that God is moved by is not impressive actions but your faith. Whether it was Abraham or the only time Jesus was ever said to be "amazed," it was in regard to people's faith. Hebrews 11:6 says, "Without faith it is impossible to please God, because anyone who comes to him must believe that he exists and that he rewards those who earnestly seek him."

As we will see later, I have been impressed that the truths and principles communicated in the Bible are far more than religious ought-to's and should's. They are laws of existence that are universal. And faith is a central principle. Your belief matters, and there is something other-worldly in its effect.

Belief goes far beyond just getting you to try harder or merely continue trying when others stop. Granted, that alone would have value. But belief changes something fundamental in the warp and woof of your existence. Those who succeed don't merely try harder. And it also goes well beyond even trying smarter.

On June 18, 1940, Winston Churchill, the then Prime Minister of the United Kingdom, stood before the House of Commons and uttered these words,

> What General Weygand called the Battle of France is over. I expect that the Battle of Britain is about to begin. Upon this battle depends the survival of Christian civilization. Upon it depends our own British life, and the long continuity of our institutions and our Empire. The whole fury and might of the enemy must very soon be turned on us. Hitler knows that he will have to break us in this Island or lose the war. If we can stand up to him, all Europe may be free and the life of the world may move forward into broad, sunlit uplands. But if we fail, then the whole world, including the United States, including all that we have known and cared for, will sink

into the abyss of a new Dark Age made more sinister, and perhaps more protracted, by the lights of perverted science. Let us therefore brace ourselves to our duties, and so bear ourselves that, if the British Empire and its Commonwealth last for a thousand years, men will still say, "This was their finest hour."

Churchill was a prolific writer and an adroit orator. But these were far more than words.

If you read the whole of his communication to the House of Commons that day, you will note that there is an honesty to the seriousness of the day. There is a clarity on the failures and the losses they had so recently experienced. While the Battle of Dunkirk just three weeks prior was considered a miracle by many, it was a miracle of escape not victory. The Allied soldiers had escaped with their lives but had to abandon almost their entire supply of tanks, vehicles, and war supplies.

Just a month prior to this speech, on May 13, 1940, Churchill had already addressed the House of Commons. It was in the midst of the onslaught of the Germans which led to the necessity of the escape at Dunkirk. His frankness then regarding the challenge was equally epic. On this date he stood before the House of Commons and declared,

> I would say to the House as I said to those who have joined this government: I have nothing to offer but blood, toil, tears and sweat. We have before us an ordeal of the most grievous kind. We have before us many, many long months of struggle and of suffering.
>
> You ask, what is our policy? I will say: It is to wage

war, by sea, land and air, with all our might and with all the strength that God can give us; to wage war against a monstrous tyranny, never surpassed in the dark and lamentable catalogue of human crime. That is our policy. You ask, what is our aim? I can answer in one word: Victory. Victory at all costs—Victory in spite of all terror—Victory, however long and hard the road may be, for without victory there is no survival...

I take up my task in buoyancy and hope. I feel sure that our cause will not be suffered to fail among men.

To some it would sound like propaganda. To Churchill it was belief. And the mark of his leadership was that it became the belief of a nation as well as a world that stood against tyranny.

For Martin Luther King, Jr', "I have a dream" was more than a vague fantasy. It was belief in the "promissory note" of freedom that the *Declaration of Independence* and the *Emancipation Proclamation* offered.

For Abraham Lincoln, the dedication of the burial ground near Gettysburg for soldiers lost in the Civil War was more than a ceremonial task. It was the same promissory note of which Martin Luther King, Jr. would speak more than a century later. Lincoln's words have literally become famous:

> Fourscore and seven years ago our fathers brought forth, on this continent, a new nation, conceived in liberty, and dedicated to the proposition that all men are created equal...

We here highly resolve that these dead shall not have died in vain – that this nation, under God, shall have a new birth of freedom, and that government of the people, by the people, for the people, shall not perish from the earth.

For Patrick Henry, "Give me liberty, or give me death!" was more than rhetoric. It was a challenge to raise a militia to defend against the British crown. It also was a challenge based on belief in the sovereignty, not long in the future, of a fledgling nation.

All of these were declarations of belief in the face of seemingly overwhelming odds. As a result, they are remembered as markers when the course of history was changed.

> There is something unique and powerful about your belief that is more than mere opinion.

There is something unique and powerful about your belief that is more than mere opinion.

Your belief matters.

## BELIEF TRANSFORMATION

### Chapter 2
Calibrate your beliefs:

- One of the greatest differences between success and failure is true belief.

- If your beliefs are detrimental, there is not enough money to overcome them.

- There are not enough obstacles to make your belief ineffective.

- There is an actual belief beyond your presumed belief that ultimately defines your future.

- Real belief works.

- There is something other-worldly in the effects of faith. True belief changes something fundamental in the warp and woof of your existence.

- Your deepest belief is unique and powerful and far more than mere opinion.

- Your belief matters.

How aware am I of my beliefs?

Do I see the influence of my beliefs on my actions?

Where are my beliefs aiding or undermining my effectiveness?

# 3

# ACQUIRE DIRECTION:
## THE POWER OF A COACH

Belief matters. But the world is full of beliefs that prove to be empty. Unrequited loves. Dreams that never materialize. Even if your belief is real, even if it is powerful, how do you engage that power?

## ETHICAL CHEATING

What if you could get unusual access to answers, artificially elevated results without it being immoral?

I don't actually believe it is okay to cheat. But I use the phrase "ethical cheating" to get your attention. "Ethical cheating" highlights the means by which you can achieve the same power and advantage many have tried to obtain through cheating while using totally ethical and moral means.

So what's the attraction and problem with cheating anyways?

The attraction of cheating is it gives you an advantage that your present lifestyle and discipline wouldn't give you. One definition of cheating is taking an examination or test by improper access to answers.[1]

Here's how one philosopher described the problem of cheating:

So why is cheating wrong?

> Most obviously, cheating is unfair to honest students. A cheater receives through deception what honest students work hard for; and in classes graded on a curve, he lowers their grades to boot. Cheating also cheapens the diploma. How valuable can a sheepskin be if so many people receive it under false pretenses?[2]

To start with, you need to understand that you are competent and have sufficient capacity for the bulk of life. Every person carries belief about his or her proficiency – including you. Even so, you do not need to live as if controlled by circumstances nor with a sense of victimization. That being true, you also need to know there are many things that are beyond anyone's paygrade.

If we have to rely solely on our own skill, or savvy, or understanding, we will regularly come up short and limit the impact of our life.

Video games have what are called secret codes or "cheats." We call them "lifehacks" in everyday life. In either case we're referring to finding easier ways to arrive at the end result by piggybacking on the ideas or experiences of others.

Life and business offer a special opportunity which is so significant and so powerful that it can elevate you beyond your contemporaries. It also will allow you to exceed anything you could accomplish otherwise. The obvious difference between those who have it and those who don't is so remarkable that it provides the same significant benefit as cheating, but without the aftertaste. In other words, it gives you the ability to achieve exponentially beyond your present competence without cheapening the results.

If you truly have this unique advantage, it gives you the ability to do business at a level far above your own personal experience, education, or understanding. It clarifies how to make critical decisions. It defines the values that order the structure of your business. It inspires you to live in a way that exceeds any personal internal drive you may have.

The secret lies in your final source of authority.

The secret lies in your final source of authority. This chapter will walk you through what this is, why you need it, and how it radically affects your life and business.

## The Power of a Coach

A decade ago I began noticing my metabolism wasn't having the same impact it use to have. Aside from ice cream and whole milk – and okay, some quarter-pounders, French-fries, frozen Snickers bars, blueberry pie, Sprite, and a few other things I won't bother to mention – I didn't really eat all that badly.

Truth be told, however, my problem wasn't that my diet

had significantly changed.

I had begun to recognize a potential need. But initially that realization did not arrest my attention sufficiently for me to do anything significant about it. Several years passed and my belt notches and our apparently malfunctioning bathroom scale began to tell a story which was so obvious I could no longer deny it.

Even so, the problem was that this still was not enough to result in any consistent overt action. Eventually I began coaching one, then two, then three, people in the health industry. In addition, a lady who had overcome cancer merely by changing how she ate joined one of our business think tanks. And finally, I started coaching an owner of a CrossFit-style gym. It took these and seven years to finally get my attention.

However, attention and effect are not the same. Before I could enjoy real change I had to actually join a CrossFit gym and spend multiple sessions each week working out and listening to the gym's owner and trainer, Levi Lee. This is in addition to the others who had been describing the benefits of eating healthy and working out properly.

Despite witnessing numerous people join workout facilities (including myself) with little effect, I now began experiencing significant results.

I'm a naturally self-motivated person, but it took having a personal trainer and people with whom I regularly worked out to create a significant visible change. My belt notches started moving in the right direction. My scale started working properly again. I even became the top performer of the gym. None of these would have happened without some kind of external challenge or impetus.

No matter how intelligent, self-motivated, or successful the person, no one can achieve alone what they can achieve with a quality coach – one that is a source of external motivation, clarification, and discipline. Often when I came away from an exercise time or gave up an unhealthy food source, it caused me to realize how great a change had transpired. I previously might have known that I was making the right move, but I would not have consistently made the right call if it had been all up to me.

In 1919 UCLA created its first basketball team. From 1919 to 1948 they compiled a very mediocre 286-283 record. But in 1948 they hired the "Wizard of Westwood," John Wooden, as their head coach. In his first year they went from being 12-13 to 22-7. The previous 50% winning percentage changed to a cumulative 81% winning percentage over Wooden's 27 years at UCLA.

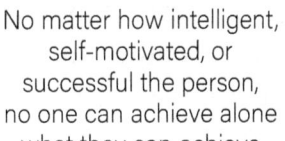

No matter how intelligent, self-motivated, or successful the person, no one can achieve alone what they can achieve with a quality coach.

In the almost 100 years of UCLA's storied basketball program, the Bruins have won 11 national championships. 10 of them were during Wooden's coaching tenure. And while his legacy has had a permanent impact on their program, at no other time has their success equaled his record.

In all of his coaching career, Wooden had only one losing season: his first coaching season when he was a 22-year-old neophyte high school basketball coach in Dayton, Kentucky. He also lost only one championship game. Again, it was his first championship while he coached the Indiana State Sycamores.

Did Wooden just get lucky across all of those successful years of coaching? Did he just happen to pick teams with better players?

People appreciate the impact of a coach, but they may not understand the reason why coaches are so powerful. Fundamentally coaches teach skills. But the great ones go far beyond that to illuminate a broader perspective than any individual player brings to the team. They inspire. They unite varying skills. They identify and implement the right timing, the right mix, and the right strategy. They have the authority to hold team members accountable. They have the authority to make final decisions. The best coaches do this not only at an external level but, even more so, at an internal level.

Sports may look primarily physical, but universally they are as much mental as they are physical. Your mind tends to give out before your body does. As it has been humorously stated, "It's mind over matter. If you don't mind, it doesn't matter." When you learn to win at the mental level, the body and the physical disciplines will follow. If you choose to execute in spite of fatigue, frustration, temptation, distractions, or disappointment, you can succeed. Great coaches create an atmosphere and instigate a challenge to live this out both on and off the court.

Coaching is a clearly observable source of authority. And while coaching has its limits, it demonstrates the impact and importance of a trustworthy mentor.

## The Necessity of Authority

The ultimate source of a coach's impact is authority. This is not particularly referring to a dictatorial type of authority – instead, it is the power of influence produced by the coach's superior grasp of the sport. The authority possessed by a good coach gives him or her the power to quickly settle issues, delegate, assign roles, define goals, authorize, institute and enforce requirements, inspire action, create calm under pressure, as well as taking the disparate ideas, abilities, and goals of the individual team member and uniting them into a cohesive whole.

The only way they have the power to do these things is if they have been given the authority to do them by the organization, plus an acceptance and commitment to that authority by the players themselves.

No matter how talented, experienced, or mature the players, they still have limited perspective, imperfect discipline. Furthermore, they often desire the wrong things. Take the most capable athlete you can think of: Michael Jordan, Mohammad Ali, Tiger Woods, Jim Thorpe, Michael Phelps, Peggy Fleming, Pele, Bobby Orr, Simone Biles, Roger Federer, or your own favorite athlete. Every one of these had a coach for as long as they competed. Although they were professionals at the peak of their sport, they still needed external input. And that input needed to hold significant sway over everything about their game.

The more powerful and trustworthy the authority, the more transformative the effect. Sports provide excellent examples because the effects are easily seen and quantified. Whenever a team lacks confidence in the authority of the coach, their game and team observably suffer.

One of the best ways to excel in any endeavor is get an external, trustworthy source of authority and do exactly what he, she, or it says. Authorities challenge, command, control, and determine courses of action. But it is when the coaching is opposed to our tendencies that its value is greatest. Yet most people spend their energy resisting authority instead of benefiting from it – especially when it challenges their natural tendencies.

I just came back from a graduation exercise at Parris Island – the Marine Corps' boot camp for new recruits. The events of the week included a commanders' banquet where friends and family were able to meet the commanders and drill instructors.

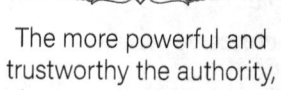

The more powerful and trustworthy the authority, the more transformative the effect.

It was an intriguing opportunity to ask questions of the drill instructors themselves – and they were very forthcoming about their own history, experience, and the purpose and extent of the process the recruits went through. It also was extremely eye-opening to sit down with one of the new Marines and get immediate feedback regarding bootcamp.

Of the several thousand recruits on the base, only a fraction are graduating at any particular time. The rest are in the midst of what this Marine called "Full Metal Jacket [the movie] times ten."

While most of the recruits are out of sight, I happened to pass a group in a sandpit who were getting what is euphemistically called IT (Incentive Training). It was led by three drill instructors – one with about six recruits and the other two with one recruit each. This is the one time you do not want personal attention.

I slowed down the car as I rolled the window down. I confess to smiling at the poor plight of those profusely sweating, absolutely exhausted recruits. It was not their day – and the DI's were doing everything they could to make sure of that. The DI's approach was a serious violation of a phrase my girls sometimes use, "Don't judge me!"

When our nation's security and the life of a Marine and his platoon are on the line, absolute authority and absolute trust are paramount. Boot camp is designed to create that understanding with a belief and trust in authority. This results in the U.S. having the most powerful military force in the world as the key to the freedoms we now enjoy.

Their willingness to follow a trustworthy authority is one of the distinguishing character qualities of those who are successful. As we earlier claimed, this commitment results in the differentiating power of cheating without the negative ethical side effects.

What most do not understand is everyone has final sources of authority in their life – that is sources of authority that they give ultimate allegiance. In the words of Bob Dylan, "You're gonna have to serve somebody."

> You may be an ambassador to England or France
> You may like to gamble, you might like to dance
> You may be the heavyweight champion of the world
> You may be a socialite with a long string of pearls
> But you're gonna have to serve somebody, yes
> Indeed you're gonna have to serve somebody

Well, it may be the devil or it may be the Lord
But you're gonna have to serve somebody

## Destructive Authority

Having given such a ringing endorsement of authority, the fact that not all authorities are productive might be surprising. In truth, the most widely adhered to authorities are destructive. They are unreliable, untrustworthy, and inconsistent. People follow them by default rather than by overt choice. They are often not a person, organization, or legal document. Although these authorities are abstract and even incoherent, they hold powerful sway over people's most serious and significant decisions.

Some of the most common sources of default authority are ego, fear, peer pressure, and undisciplined desire. These constantly affect and often distort the business and life choices of the typical business person. Most are blissfully unaware that they have given absolute allegiance to these authorities – and that these default, yet distorted authorities, are calling most of the shots in their lives.

On November 4, 1979, a group of Iranian students stormed the U.S. Embassy in Tehran, taking 66 Americans hostage. Many believe this was a pivotal issue in President Reagan's election over then President Carter. Herb Cohen, a top-level negotiator was brought in by Carter to give him advice on what to do. Unfortunately, Cohen's advice was mostly ignored by Carter. So on Oct. 25, 1980, Cohen expressed his perspective on this situation in a confidential memo to candidate Reagan.

In his memo Cohen explained why he believed Reagan would win the election and how that would result with the hostages being released at the time of the transition of power. Just as Cohen predicted, on January 21, 1981 – a few hours after Reagan's inauguration speech – as if on cue, the hostages were released.

Most are blissfully unaware that they have given absolute authority to these authorities.

In his book, *Negotiate This!*, Cohen writes:

> In the intervening years, I have been asked numerous times "How were you able to analyze this matter and foretell the outcome with such certainty?" My best answer is that, unlike others whose intellect and intelligence were superior, I didn't have a career or reputation invested in the crisis. And I was less inhibited by a desire for acceptance or fear of disapproval.[3]

My two daughters are transitioning between their teens and twenties. I am often reminded of my own journey during this same time of life. No matter how well-connected we are with our parents, there always is the desire to fully determine the direction of our own lives. It isn't just the rebellious young person that attempts to step away from parental authority into that authority which they see as being connected to adulthood. All of us undergo this transition.

Universally, there is the assumption that this "grabbing the bull by the horns" equates to becoming our own authority. What many never grasp, however, is that you never become free from some source of authority. You may be ignorant of the exact source, but you are not devoid of it. This is powerfully true in business.

The most significant authorities that are at play in your present business setting are not the ones you might first be inclined to identify. Instead, often unrecognized internal sources of authority exert the greatest influence.

You are constantly, even actively, choosing what authorities will have the greatest weight in your life. It may be external authorities of bosses, clients, governmental regulations, economic indicators or trends. It may be emotionally connected realities like deadlines, mandatory goals, or crises. It may be the heart level authorities referred to earlier of ego, fear, peer pressure, aspirations, or desire. Whatever the real authorities may be, even if they are inappropriate, they often determine your choices.

That means you can more adequately choose who or what will stand in their place by understanding their existence and their power. If you choose well - and a good coach can be a key resource - the power of the right authority can have its most beneficial and differentiating effect.

> Often unrecognized internal sources of authority exert the greatest influence.

Even more, if you understand the same is true for employees, clients, suppliers, the clerk at the apparently bureaucratic government agency, or even the cashier at the grocery store, you will have a unique insight into what motivates people. Discover what their authority is and you will understand the things that drive their lives. Identify these and you uncover their fundamental motivators. Indeed, it is beyond simple motivation, for it is a decision-maker.

Identifying your own final source of authority is an even more important insight. This allows you to uncover your true and deepest motivating factors.

# BELIEF TRANSFORMATION

## Chapter 3
Calibrate your beliefs:

- The secret to achieving results that outstrip your present experience, study, and discipline is found in your final source of authority.

- No matter how intelligent, self-motivated, or successful the person, no one can achieve alone what they can achieve with a quality coach.

- Coaching is a clearly observable source of authority.

- One of the best ways to excel is get an external, trustworthy source of authority and follow precisely what he, she, or it says.

- Coaching has its greatest value when it is opposed to our tendencies.

- Everyone has final sources of authority in their life – sources of authority that they give ultimate allegiance.

- The most widely adhered to authorities are destructive. They are unreliable, untrustworthy, and inconsistent. The most common of which are ego, fear, peer pressure, and undisciplined desire.

- Most are blissfully unaware they have given absolute allegiance to these default authorities.

## ACQUIRE DIRECTION

- Uncovering your or other's final source of authority allows you to uncover your or their true and deepest motivating factors.

Have I been attempting to pursue life without the benefit of external authority or coaching?

What is my natural response to coaching or authority specifically when it challenges my tendencies?

Where is my best opportunity for advantageous coaching?

# 4

# ACHIEVE EXTREME ADVANTAGE:
## ESTABLISH YOUR SOURCE OF AUTHORITY

### THE CHALLENGE OF BEING A SOPHOMORE

If you have children, grandchildren, nieces, or nephews, you know the challenge of explaining what is beyond their ability to grasp. To some young children, roads appear like perfect places to play and antifreeze looks like Kool-Aid. No matter how accurate or well-intended, your input is unsolicited and often unwelcomed.

Watch their reaction when you correct their perceptions! As a result, initially you merely aim for obedience. Recognizing they are not going to understand why, we often resort to "Because I told you!" All parents should come to the realization that the question "Why?" is merely a stalling or bargaining tactic. Children really don't care why you said they shouldn't eat candy before dinner.

"Absolutely, mother. I'm glad I asked, why. I had other plans. Now, having understood that my nutritional health is at a premium, I will forgo this sweet-tasting candy to instead indulge in my broccoli," said no child ever.

Even adults are resistant when faced with new concepts. We all need a final source of authority.

Several years ago, a family moved into our neighborhood. The father had a job that required him to be out of town more than at home. The mother had come to an unstated agreement with her son that the structure of the home was basically "live and let live."

A friend of our family had this son in a high school class. An assignment was given to write an essay on the students' house rules. After class his candid response was that he couldn't do the assignment. "We don't have any house rules."

Soon after this, while coming back from running with my oldest daughter, I saw him lean into the window of a car that had pulled up to his house. I watched with interest as they made a quick exchange and the car sped off.

I asked my daughter, "Did you see that? He just sold that guy some drugs!"

I was already aware of the reason for the increased traffic to our neighbor's house. Even though he was in a quality neighborhood, along with one of the best school districts in the nation, the outcome of his life was clearly on a death spiral.

A few months later, I got a call from his mother frantically asking for help to get her son out of jail. Now she had to deal with a crisis she had never anticipated.

She was an exception to what most parents understand: the challenge youth face in making decisions for which they are not adequately prepared.

We even recognize this by the way we label high school and college grade levels: freshmen, sophomore and junior. These all connote a sense of immaturity or naiveté.

The word sophomore is especially interesting. It is derived from two Greek words: *sophos moros*. *Sophos* means wise; *moros* is the word from which we get moron. Sophomore literally means, "wise-fool." What a perfect description of having just enough knowledge to be dangerous.

What sophomores don't realize is as we mature, instead of becoming obliviously self-assured, we become more aware of the difference between what we know and what we don't know. The most mature realize how much they need to rely on others. They have progressed from dependency to greater independence to a pursuit of being interdependent.

While learning to pursue sources of information and excellence, few understand the value – and the power – of having an absolutely trustworthy final source of authority.

I'm not sure we ever fully grow up. But when we continue to develop throughout the course of our lives, we keep growing. If we continue to advance, we grow both in self-confidence and in understanding of our own limitations – and therefore about our need of others.

Sophomore literally means "wise-fool."

The most mature among us also discover their need of an authority (a clarifier of what is true) greater than themselves and their own limited experience.

## The Challenge of Finding a Trustworthy Authority

In our culture many see a lack of self-esteem as one of our most serious issues. I'm not convinced the evidence backs up that observation. Having become enamored with our advanced knowledge, we conclude our scientific development has caused us to know what is true, right, ethical and productive.

This perceived wisdom may be based on some of society's recent accomplishments. Nevertheless, the malady of unfounded self-confidence has always existed.

Our technological advances allow us to get rapid, clear feedback. However, it doesn't reveal wisdom, ethics and truth – our ultimate needs.

Some may cite universal agreement as a means of satisfying this need. If everyone agreed – especially if they agreed for centuries – that would be a good sign. But it is not a guarantee – many things which were once widely agreed upon have later turned out to be totally wrong or seriously insufficient.

In fact, we still find significant disagreement regarding many issues. When the brightest and wisest minds don't agree, what does that reveal about our ability to adequately know the truth?

In the United States our ultimate trust is in our Constitution, representative democracy, and three separate but equal branches of government. We have a constitution that is enacted by a legislature, enforced by an executive branch, and ultimately interpreted by a supreme court.

The members of the Supreme Court are not just called lawyers, i.e., people of the law. They are referred to as "justices" – implying their decisions are just. Numerous decisions by this court are unanimous. This is encouraging until you get to the most significant decisions.

Look at 10 of the landmark decisions of our Supreme Court – sited at random without prejudice or regard to the outcome.

*Brown v. Board of Education of Topeka*, 1954 (passed 9-0). Segregation was outlawed – but only after much discussion because this court ruling overturned the *Plessy v. Ferguson* decision of another Supreme Court. Those "justices" had ruled in the opposite direction in 1896 by a 7-1 margin. This was one of several times in which a subsequent Supreme Court had overruled an earlier decision by a different set of "justices."

*Mapp v. Ohio*, 1961 (passed 6-3). It was ruled that illegally obtained evidence cannot be used.

*Engel v. Vitale*, 1962 (passed 6-1). This decision declared official school prayer in public schools was unconstitutional.

*Baker v. Carr*, 1962 (passed 6-2-1). Electoral districts must be apportioned according to population; so that each person is given an equal vote. This issue was so problematic that they couldn't come to a decision for a year.

*Miranda v. Arizona*, 1966 (passed 5-4). The accused were given their "Miranda rights."

*Roe v. Wade*, 1973 (passed 7-2). The court ruled that a

woman's right to privacy under the Due Process Clause of the 14th Amendment extended to a woman's decision to have an abortion.

*Texas v. Johnson*, 1989 (passed 5-4). People were given the right to desecrate our national flag.

*Cruzan v. Director, Missouri Dept. of Health*, 1990 (passed 5-4). This was known as "the right to die" ruling. A patient's wish for the removal of life support became acceptable upon "clear and convincing evidence" that the patience concurred.

*Bush v. Gore*, 2000 (passed 7-2/5-4). These two rulings ultimately certified the vote of the Florida electorate. This resulted in Bush winning Florida's 25 electoral votes, and thereby, the Presidency.

*Obergefell v. Hodges*, 2015 (passed 5-4). This court decision legalized gay marriage.

Quite aside from any emotional reactions these decisions may produce, these are ten significant rulings. Consider this brief overview of the results.

First, these are decisions of our nation's "Supreme Court" – supposedly the best, wisest, most trusted court. If we ever get true justice, this should be the place.

Second, of these ten rulings, only one was unanimous. This unanimous decision overturned a previous, almost equally unanimous, decision by a different Supreme Court. This means that judges often totally disagree about matters which are supposed to reflect true justice under the Constitution.

Third, the average decision was 6-3. This is far from unanimous agreement among people who were selected for their ability to rule wisely. In fact, some of the most important decisions by the Supreme Court have hinged on a single "swing vote." Obviously, the decision of a single "justice" is hardly a reliable way to determine what is right and just – particularly when four other "justices" have reached exactly the opposite conclusion after considering precisely the same information.

Finally, it frequently is well understood – prior to the actual decision – in which direction many of the individual "justices" will vote. As much as they would like to claim otherwise, their rulings largely reflect much more of the personal biases of the individuals than "blind justice." Clearly, when many crucial decisions are being made, there often are significant disagreements among nine people who are alleged to be among "the best and the brightest."

Sometimes even when individual "justices" agree with one side or the other, they may prepare different explanations of why they either agree or disagree with the ruling. So even the final vote may not reveal all the differences in perspective on what is right and just.

The bottom line – we have justice issues which indicate deep reality challenges. It is not a fluke that the Supreme Court frequently struggles with defining what is consistent with the Constitution. This is not to denigrate the court, but to illuminate an issue of truth and authority that extends far beyond our country's Supreme Court.

We have authority issues. They didn't stop when we graduated from our teen years. We instinctively know we need authority – yet when we are forced to comply, we innately dislike doing so.

A child often does not choose their final source of authority. An adult supposedly can. What is yours? Do you know?

In 1789 the Constitutional Convention established our country's Constitution. But from a personal standpoint there are two relevant questions:

What have you established as the primary governing source of your decisions?

How did you conclude this is your governing source?

Among the most common final sources of authority are: universal or majority agreement (social norms), instinct or gut feeling, governmental law (the Constitution, Supreme Court rulings, legislation), the Bible or other authoritative religious writings, logic (whether personal logic or some other source you recognize as logical), spiritual awareness, experience, internal desire, or a mix of some of these.

In all likelihood you recognize multiple authorities. You may see several of these as being significant. But what or who is the arbiter when there is disagreement? Which is your final authority? The biases of the individual justices illustrate why you need to fully understand what authorities motivate or determine the decisions you make.

The reality is whenever you make a decision, even if you don't recognize it, it is always an authority-based decision. Most don't have a black or white understanding of the authorities that motivate or even determine their decisions. As you more completely grasp what is true about the authorities of your life, you will more completely understand how and why you are making your decisions.

I'm not primarily referring to external authorities that

most think of when they hear the word authority. The authorities influencing the decisions people make are internal, gut-level authorities. These authorities define their belief systems and are fundamental to their worldview.

Most college students are woefully unprepared for college. Whether they can make the grades may present its own challenges. Their real weakness is they understand neither what they believe nor what their beliefs are founded on. As a result, they are easy targets for whatever their professors or the prevalent culture promotes.

> Whenever you make a decision, even if you don't recognize it, it is always an authority-based decision.

How does this same deficit in identifying your own underlying sources of authority affect your business performance? And what if you have chosen inadequate sources of authority?

## The Power of a Final Source of Authority

David, the most highly regarded and successful king in the history of Israel in all likelihood wrote Psalm 119. Here is an excerpt:

> [97] Oh, how I love your law! I meditate on it all day long. [98] Your commands are always with me and make me wiser than my enemies. [99] I have more insight than all my teachers, for I meditate on your statutes. [100] I have more understanding than the elders, for I obey your precepts. [101] I have kept my feet from every evil path so that I might obey your word. [102] I have not departed from your laws,

for you yourself have taught me. [103] How sweet are your words to my taste, sweeter than honey to my mouth! [104] I gain understanding from your precepts; therefore I hate every wrong path. [105] Your word is a lamp for my feet, a light on my path.

It is odd to think of loving laws. Laws are necessary but definitely not on the top of the list of the things we love. Speed limits always seem slower than they need to be. The autobahn without a speed limit seems appealing. Seatbelts are annoying unless we begrudgingly admit they may very well save lives. And who really comes to a complete stop at a stop sign?

Yet King David declares that he loves God's laws. His reason? They make him wiser than his enemies, with more insight than his teachers, and greater understanding than his elders. In the business sector David's perspective applies to you versus your competitors, peers, mentors, or bosses. Every good law presses you toward what is right, productive and valuable.

> While continuing to learn may be inspiring, this is an admission of the limitations of what we know.

Because none of us has all knowledge, we all need a final source of authority. Opinions are as changeable as the wind. New information continues to adjust how we see the world – which includes business, leadership, relationships, and life in general.

The greatest leaders never stop learning. While continuing to learn may be inspiring, this is an admission of the limitations of what we know – or else we wouldn't need to always keep exploring and learning. Besides that, the best not only keep learning, they focus on very specific areas. Broad learning is helpful, but true mastery requires focus.

Malcolm Gladwell postulated the 10,000 Hour Rule. He declares that 10,000 hours of deliberate practice are necessary to become world-class in any field. If that is even remotely accurate, the number of areas in which you can actually become world-class is very limited. Furthermore, world-class doesn't mean you are perfect – just uncommonly good.

Consider just three random areas: [1] how to discipline children, [2] how to lead a business, and [3] what is healthy. How many changes to your beliefs regarding these three areas have occurred during your lifetime?

Even in one small part of the third area – namely the artificial sweetener craze – opinions have varied widely. Are they carcinogenic? Do they help or hinder weight loss? A brief overview of the research shows serious disagreement, even today. Wherever you come down on any issue, each alternative perspective has been dogmatically declared.

If that candid observation doesn't give your self-confidence pause, you're not paying attention.

Who or what do you trust? Having confidence is critical. Having confidence in what is true is far better. King David had found the ultimate trustworthy authority. It was the differentiating factor between his life, leadership, and ultimate success in comparison to everyone else.

He saw the Bible as an absolute trustworthy source of authority that clarifies truth and reality at a higher level than his own understanding. He trusted what it said absolutely. And it made all the difference.

Jim Collins writes in *Built to Last* that one of the key underlying variables that allows a company to not only go from good to great but to stay great and become an iconic institution is that they have an underlying set of core values, a guiding framework, that does not change. What are your core values? Where does your guiding framework come from?

## Confidence of Biblical Proportions

They say there are two things you don't want to see made: sausage and legislation. I have watched legislation made, and so I'm taking their word on sausage.

I was sitting in on a county commissioners meeting that was attempting to establish a ruling on zoning ordinances. They were concerned about the effect of traffic flow and their regular inability to confirm whether there would be sufficient arterial, collector, and local roadways to handle the traffic. At present there was a non-profit that was wanting to expand in a fairly residential area. The challenge was the commissioners clearly hadn't done their homework or at minimum the information gathered wasn't sufficient. They had a lot of concerns but little clarity.

They had done no or only cursory traffic studies, had no idea how much traffic various size roadways could handle, and had not thought through how differing types of businesses affect traffic flow at different times. And now they were being challenged with making a decision. Apparently this was not their first foray into this dilemma. So in their frustration, they decided they needed to come up with a zoning ordinance that specified where certain types of businesses could be built. Having a law in place would take this recurring frustration off their hands.

Just prior to taking a vote on a motion for this new ordinance, they opened up the floor for discussion. I raised my hand and asked.

"So let me get this straight. You haven't done sufficient traffic studies for this area. You don't know how much additional flow these new businesses will create. But you have a lot of pressure from the community regarding the expanding non-profit, and this is not the first time you have faced this challenge. So out of frustration you are going to cement your ignorance by making a zoning ordinance that has to be followed whether it makes real sense or not."

This was followed by an uncomfortable silence where they blinked, looked at each other, and then tabled the decision.

Sources of authority are incredibly helpful in making decisions, but if the source of my authority isn't smarter than I am or doesn't have a perspective greater than mine, then it is of little value. In fact, it becomes a silly game with potentially dire consequences.

Most people see the Bible as an ethical code book describing what is right or wrong. But the purpose of the Bible is not to help Santa Claus determine who is naughty and nice. The Bible is a declaration of what is true. This is lifesaving at a level most of us have never really considered.

Consider again how many things and societal beliefs have changed in your lifetime. It is potential, for the first time in the history of the world we have finally come to a perfect understanding of what is true, just, productive, healthy, economically and relationally accurate. It is more likely, as in all other times, we are attempting to build on our mix of experience and ignorance to make a better society.

The fact that there are still intense cultural and political divides ought to give us pause. We have not reached a state of intellectual nirvana. Who is right? To get more specific to your business, how do you determine your core values? How do you determine how you interact with the corporate culture you work within? How do you define your objectives, strategies, and priorities? Having an absolutely reliable final source of authority is critical.

Aside from what all the other competing voices may believe to be true, if I know undeniably that something is destructive, it changes my responsibility and it guides the goal of my future actions. Granted, there continues to be a significant challenge on how to live out this understanding. But when you know what is best, you can confidently determine what the goal should be.

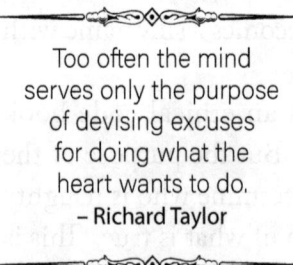

Too often the mind serves only the purpose of devising excuses for doing what the heart wants to do.
– Richard Taylor

Passion and pressure can easily distort our grasp of reality. But strong desire doesn't change reality. And pressure doesn't change what is true.

Richard Taylor in his powerful book on discipline put it this way, "Too often the mind serves only the purpose of devising excuses for doing what the heart wants to do.[1]"

Clarifying your final source of authority is the most

fundamental and significant step in defining the right response to existing challenges. What is yours? And what does it say? Establish the proper final source of authority and it provides the ultimate basis for your belief and actions.

If you can properly define your final source of authority, you will give yourself an extreme advantage by significantly differentiating your choices from the culture around you – and you will do so ethically.

# BELIEF TRANSFORMATION

## Chapter 4
Calibrate your beliefs:

- It is universal human nature to resist authority.

- There is value, even power, in having an absolutely trustworthy final source of authority.

- Productive final sources of authority counteract our internal sophomoric nature - our tendency toward being wise fools.

- The best authorities are accurate clarifiers of what is true.

- Our technological advances allow us to get rapid, clear feedback. However, they don't reveal wisdom, ethics and truth – our ultimate needs.

- Finding a fully trustworthy source of authority is harder and rarer than we may grasp.

- Decisions are always authority-based decisions.

- The authorities influencing the decisions people make are mostly internal gut-level authorities – not external.

- King David declared his differentiating factor was his love and obedience of an absolute trustworthy source of authority – God's law.

- The Bible is not fundamentally an ethical code book. Rather, it is a declaration of what is true.
- Passion and pressure easily distort our grasp of reality.
- Clarifying your final source of authority is the most fundamental and significant step in defining the right response to existing challenges.

What are your core values?

What have you established as the primary governing source of your decisions?

How do you know you have an accurate understanding of your source?

What is your final source of authority? Do you know?

# 5

# Confirm What is True:
## THE BIBLE DOES NOT APPLY TO BUSINESS

The Bible does not apply to business.

I mean this literally, just not for the reason you may assume.

## Beyond Applying

The primary dictionary definition of the word "apply" speaks of making something "relevant."[1] The connotation would often be that something is taken out of its original environment and made to work in another suitable setting. For example, applied sciences connect science to real world practice. Pure science, on the other hand, primarily speaks of scientific research to support or disprove various theories. It normally includes a closed system with limited variables.[1]

Innovations apply pure science to real life. Real life involves open systems and almost unlimited variables. While the interaction between pure and applied sciences is feasible, achievable, and highly compatible, there is still a transition that must be navigated between the two.

I would challenge you that this is not the case with the Bible. The Bible does not apply to business; it subsumes business. It encapsulates everything involved in business. Business is but a small subset of the existence described by the Bible.

It would be accurate to say the Bible defines the laws of gravity in business - the most fundamental laws of existence. The question isn't whether the Bible will work in business. The question is whether business will work according to the truth of existence as clarified in the Bible.

## Risky Belief

The almost universal assumption is that what gets talked about in church on the weekend has difficulty being translated into our weekday environment. Taking your belief into the workplace is risky because not everyone believes like you do. In this chapter you will discover that this never needs to be the issue – at least if you are working for a company which pursues excellence.

This is a risky chapter specifically because it will unequivocally clarify how and why the foundation of every one of the concepts in this book has a biblical foundation.

No matter whether you believe in God – more specifically that Jesus Christ was God – or whether you would consider yourself atheistic, agnostic, New Age, a follower of one of the eleven other classical world religions, or any other belief system, this chapter is potentially the most life-changing part of this book.

While my greatest passion would be for you to experience a true personal relationship with Jesus and the God that created you, this chapter's focus is to clarify how and why the Bible is a powerful tool for the most successful, significant, and impactful business you could create.

This is true whether you are a sole proprietor, corporate executive in a publicly traded company, governmental/public official, non-profit or religious leader. It's even true if you don't accept the God who inspired it. As you will discover, you don't have to worry about the separation of church and state or any other supposed conflict of religious belief in a secular or pluralistic society.

I would note that while I am not encouraging you to hide the source of your beliefs, neither must you always tout their source in order to be fully faithful to them. In contrast to our fear that biblical truth is inappropriate in the workplace, the reality is the truth defined in the Bible works. Its accuracy to life is exact.

The Bible isn't describing what it discovered to be true. It is clarifying what is true. If you understand what it is clarifying, in the words previously quoted from King David it can transform the excellence of what you do.

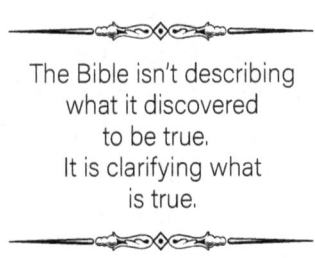

The Bible isn't describing what it discovered to be true. It is clarifying what is true.

Your commands are always with me and make me wiser than my enemies [competition]. I have more insight than all my teachers [professors or peers], for I meditate on your statutes. I have more understanding than the elders [mentors], for I obey your precepts." Psalm 119:98-100 NIV [bracketed words added]

The tendency will be to assume this is merely a religious statement of belief. It is actually just an accurate statement. In this chapter you will discover the most powerful example of the kind of final source of authority described in the previous chapter, "Achieve Extreme Advantage."

## LEADERSHIP PRINCIPLE BREADCRUMBS

I first began to realize the powerful connection between what the Bible was teaching and what business was attempting to achieve while studying leadership in graduate school.

Warren Bennis and Burt Nanus wrote a very readable book on leadership, *Leadership: The Strategies for Taking Charge*. As a foundation for the concepts of the book, they did a series of ninety interviews – thirty Fortune 200 companies, thirty successful mid-sized companies, and thirty outstanding leaders in the public sector (coaches, leaders of non-profits, governmental leaders, etc.). They describe the outcome of their research.

"It was a search for similarities in a wildly diverse group… There were more variations than themes." The authors further described the vastness of the variations in size, leadership, communication style, education, and more. "For those of us interested in pattern, in underlying themes, this group was frustratingly unruly."

At which point they concluded, "The only surprise worth mentioning is that almost all were married to their first spouse. And not only that: they were also indefatigably enthusiastic about marriage as an institution."[2]

That is an odd observation. Undoubtedly it had to stand out significantly in order to be observed because it was a surprise and not something one would normally talk about when referring to business leadership. Interestingly, Bennis and Nanus made what appeared to be a universal shrug and then continued on. Clearly they didn't know what to do with this finding.

Having significant background in theological studies I understand why Paul wrote a letter to Timothy, a young leader in the Roman city of Ephesus. Paul was the primary apostle to the gentile (non-Jewish) world in the early Church and author of thirteen of the New Testament books in the Bible. Timothy's challenge was to establish leadership in a very hostile and challenging environment.

In 1 Timothy 3, Paul describes to Timothy what to look for in leaders. Prominent in his description is the very thing that Bennis and Nanus discovered to be true in the most successful leaders – a high commitment to and successful leadership of one's spouse and family.

Previously I had assumed that Paul's directions to Timothy could basically be summarized as: filter out the ethical from the non-ethical candidates for leadership. I supposed Paul's descriptors were merely to establish clarity on the necessity of the morality of leaders – obviously a very important character trait for church leaders. I began to discover Paul was actually describing leadership – period. While not all leaders are successful at every aspect he describes, if a person is a high-end leader, they will manifest most of the characteristics Paul describes.

As I reexamined Paul's list of characteristics, I discovered a list of disciplines and character qualities that were hallmarks of effective leaders. This caused me to stop and take a second look at numerous other areas I had previously read with an eye only to one's personal life. What I discovered changed my understanding of the connection of God, the Bible, and business.

## Above Your Paygrade

The Bible is a declaration of what is true. As a result, it is an absolute, trustworthy filter and guide to what will work versus what will ultimately backfire.

Consider what you would pay for a consultant, conference, book or degree that would accurately promote itself as 100% reliable. That probably sounds like a sales pitch because absolute reliability is a fantasy in the world as we know it. Yet it is the assertion the Bible makes. If it works for business, it would be life-changing.

In the past, you may have considered what the Bible says to be a lot like this little toddler, Abby, considered her mommy.

Mommy: What's a cow say?
Abby: Moooo!
Mommy: Good! What's a pig say?

## CONFIRM WHAT IS TRUE

Abby: Oink, oink!
Daddy: What's Mommy say?
Abby: No, no, nooo!

For little Abby, having a mother is essential, beneficial, life-changing – and in her mind, a regular kill-joy.

Consider a different perspective in regard to the Bible. To put it in bullet-point conciseness, the following is a peek behind the curtain as to the value and power of the Bible as a final source of authority:

- You have limited knowledge and wisdom.
- Where the accuracy of your knowledge and wisdom stop, your productivity and impact fade.
- Congruence with truth is productive. Incongruence is ultimately destructive – always.
- The Bible declares what is true, not merely what is ethical or good.
- If you have absolute clarity on what is true, you have a roadmap to success and an unequaled leg up on your competition.
- If you have absolute clarity on what is true, you can distinguish fad from reliable business principle.
- If you have complete confidence in your source of authority, you can follow its guidance even if the why is above your paygrade.

The last point is probably the most beneficial – but also

the most resisted. Where we most need authoritative direction is where we are painfully clueless. Even when we don't understand the underlying reasoning, if we trust the source, we will follow it anyway.

We have all kinds of assumptions that are inaccurate. Oddly enough, the accuracy of our assumptions is often unrelated to the tenacity with which we hold them.

## OUR WORDS TELL ON US

During a review of third quarter performance you are called into the president's office. She gives you this rather unsubtle piece of information, "I've taken a close look at our sales, receivables, cash flow, and projected earnings, so let me be frank with you. We have to really watch the bottom line this last quarter."

> The accuracy of our assumptions is often unrelated to the tenacity with which we hold them.

Although it doesn't rise to the level of rocket science – what does she mean by "bottom line?"

Shortly afterward, you come home to a family including two little kids – one, a toddler, and the other trying to get out of diapers – literally. He's running circles in the kitchen giggling and screaming with his diaper half on and half off. Your spouse starts thinking out loud. "You know it's really hitting home that we have more than ourselves to think about now. We want our kids growing up in a great, stable environment."

As you chase down the escaping diaper villain, you hear the tail end of her audible thoughts, "We really need to work on the spiritual side of our lives."

What did she mean "spiritual side?"

Did you catch it – the words we use? The words we use have significant implications.

When we speak of the "bottom line" we are referring to the Success level being the most important consideration. Unfortunately we are also relegating our Soul level to the "sideline" – the spiritual side. I know we don't mean it that way – at least not out loud or even by our conscious thoughts. Even so, the words we use tell on us.

The Success we seek is great as a tool – but it is destructive as a driving force if it has become our *raison d'être* – our reason for being, our true "bottom line." And the Soul level, the truly valuable source of Why – which should be behind everything – has become our afterthought or at best an intramural activity.

So where do we go wrong? How did we get upside down and sideways? How do we affect the way we think? If I'm naturally predisposed to want and even trust what is tangible, how can I substantively change what is so completely instinctive within me? Or am I chasing after a mirage?

Unless you fundamentally change what you believe you can't pull this transition off. And that fundamental transition of belief doesn't happen magically. But there is something amazing that happens if you begin by being willing to risk leveraging what you have in order to achieve what is potential but exponentially greater.

## Counterintuitive

The word "counterintuitive" was coined in the mid-1950's and became a buzzword in the next decade. In essence this word refers to "ideas contrary to common-sense assumptions."[3] We have come to realize that there are many critical concepts which are diametrically opposed to what we commonly assume to be true. So we coined a word to describe this phenomenon. The counterintuitive may be intriguing, but when reality is counter to our intuition or heartfelt belief, we often will resist and even be inclined to reject reality.

How do you know if concepts counter to your gut or the prevailing opinion are counterintuitive or just foolish?

Leadership principles are numerous and not always consistent. How do you pick which ones you will implement? And once you choose one to implement, how confident are you in its ultimate effectiveness?

You probably understand that the most beneficial concepts normally require significant investment prior to experiencing beneficial results. Consequently, you will often be heavily invested in a concept or process before you appreciate if it truly has value. It is a painful and costly experience to travel down a long, arduous road only to find it just leads to an expensive and exhausting dead end.

Our outlook about our ability to ultimately understand what is productive tends to be overly positive. We often title our positive thinking as R&D – research and development. Truth is our R&D is often much more like T&E – trial and error. Beyond that, many concepts, when halfheartedly pursued, end up with meager results. Only when you give abandoned, consistent, tenacious commitment over an extended period of time does your attitude create its full impact. If you don't have significant trust in the potential viability of what you are attempting, it may be impossible to apply this kind of disciplined pursuit.

What if you had a source that could dramatically improve your clarity prior to heading down the T&E road – a source that you fully trusted?

If you have a trustworthy final source of authority – one that defines reality and is a grid you can lay over opportunities - that authority would inspire valuable confidence, even prior to personal experience.

## My Pleasure

Gary was in his early- to mid-20's. He had great potential which had already been displayed in several key endeavors.

I asked him a question I have referred to many times in mentoring and in leadership settings. It's a question that is as valid for a 50 or 60-year-old as it is for a 20-something or even a teenager. Unfortunately, this question often produces the sensation of an ego challenge. My question to Gary was, "Tell me, how you honor your parents." It elicited a befuddled look followed by a rather incredulous response along the lines, "How old do you I think I am?"

I ask this question because of its tremendous value. Gary's reaction revealed a detrimental attitude which was affecting his potential in leadership endeavors.

What does how you honor your parents have to do with anyone who is an adult, fully independent, and functioning on their own? Everything.

One of the key lessons my father taught me about what made him so successful in his business leadership was his commitment to respect people. If you want to lead people, you have to respect them. You may have to call them on the carpet and even chew them out. But if you want to have true impact, they must know that you respect them. Being able to chew someone out – even as they, deep inside, know you have respect for them – may sound like an oxymoron. But it is doable and highly effective.

Dee Ann Turner, Vice-President of Corporate Talent for Chick-fil-A, writes regarding the culture of her company:

> Several key actions consistently executed in Chick-fil-A restaurants have contributed to a culture that supports the promise that everyone should be treated with honor, dignity, and respect. These include the response of "My pleasure," making Second-Mile Service second nature and creating remarkable experiences for guests. The actions help create and strengthen a compelling culture among guests.

This attitude is encouraged throughout the organization, not just standing at the counter in a local restaurant. She continues:

> Service makes people feel honored, respected and special... behaviors become a natural part of the core of the organization internally and then are demonstrated externally to guests.[4]

The entire culture of Chick-fil-A is to be honoring toward each other. They are not talking about a politically correct or politically motivated attempt to avoid legal entanglements. It is not a spineless inability to have candid conversations. Rather, it is a gut level attitude that changes the way people interact with each other.

I shared Turner's declaration about Chick-fil-A's culture of honor with a leader of another organization. Her eyes brightened as she related how she had personally seen their culture in action.

She had a meeting at the Chick-fil-A headquarters with one of their vice-presidents. When the vice-president came out to meet her, his response to the receptionist was so unique that it caught her attention. In her words, he treated the receptionist as if she were just as valuable to the success of the organization as he was. His respect for the receptionist was palpable.

Take this one step further. Two key things businesses are looking to establish are an excellent image and repeat customers. How do you establish these? One crucial source is excellence in customer service. With most businesses, customer service is done as a means of solidifying the bottom line. In other words, customer service is pursued only as much as it is beneficial to the bottom line.

Customer service done with this motivation is merely customer manipulation. If your primary motive is just wanting more of your customers' money, you are not really serving them. You are manipulating them. If you do not know how to honor others, if respecting others is not part of your character, you are ill-equipped to provide true customer service. Again, you may be adept at customer manipulation, but it is next to impossible to build a culture of customer service without understanding honor at the heart level.

Turner further explains:

> Most importantly, "It's My Pleasure!" is only the language we have chosen to express the spirit of gratitude we have for our guests and an opportunity to serve them.[5]

How do you establish this kind of corporate culture? The most powerful way to create a culture of honor and respect is to proactively hire people who are that way already.

A secondary, more reactive, and less productive way is to do the hard work of inspiring honor – or if all else fails, requiring it. Just think of the massive issues with sexual harassment, workplace violence, and challenges of gender, racial or other inequalities. Many have been mistreated in these ways. Some have attempted to use the cultural backlash against these to vent a disgruntled attitude. But if your culture is saturated with honor, it is difficult for these issues to arise or find traction.

*You may be adept at customer manipulation, but it is next to impossible to build a culture of customer service without understanding honor at the heart level.*

What makes the difference between those who are honoring and those who are clueless? What may surprise you is many times you need look no further than how they honor their parents.

Psychologists and sociologists understand that your formative years define much of your life. Even despots like Vladimir Lenin got this. He said, "Give me just one generation of youth, and I'll transform the whole world." The reality of relational laws is that, like gravity, anyone can benefit from them. The question is do you understand them. Our present culture is attempting to force civility, oddly enough, even by uncivil means. There is a better way.

## Universal Effect

The Ten Commandments are basically made up of four commandments on how to love God and six on how to love people. The very first commandment on how to love people says this, *"Honor your father and your mother, so that you may live long in the land the LORD your God is giving you* (Exodus 20:12)." If you want to develop an ability to excel at leadership, learn to excel in respect and honor. If you want to learn to respect and honor, go back to the first place you had to learn to do so – with your parents.

Let me reiterate, the Bible does not apply to business; it subsumes business. It does not merely give concepts or ideas. It defines what is true. This makes it the most powerful and accessible source of business development. Honoring your parents may seem unnecessary, archaic, or even restrictive. But it creates fundamental character that results in life and business success. What you do or did in regard to your parents is not even on the radar of our corporate development. And yet it should be. Or course, if you don't care about the success of your business, feel free to ignore this principle. If you want to transform the impact of what you are doing, take a second look.

What initially looks like an unrelated principle for children and families is actually a law of relational connections which is defining the character of many successful businesses. Again, since this, like gravity, is a universal law, it works regardless of your personal or stated corporate beliefs.

Those who work in a corporate, public, or governmental setting don't have to legislate that people read the Bible in order to benefit from the power of these concepts. If you personally understand the Bible's laws of economy – and incorporate them into your business practices and policies – you can benefit from them no matter what people's religious beliefs are.

By placing your absolute confidence in them, you can intuitively promote them in your business setting. And you can do all of this without referring to the source of your brilliance. I would encourage you to be open with your belief. But no matter what you or your corporate setting states as its beliefs, the concepts of the Bible work if you follow them.

Most successful businesses have at least partially caught on to many of these concepts. They may be mixed in with a number of other less trustworthy commitments. Unfortunately, they may also be officially promoted but not actually enacted – remember Enron?

Even so, at some level most businesses would accept them as valuable. If you trust the Bible as your final source of authority, you just happen to be aware of how essential they are. You also know what to look for in potential leaders, how to better approach customers, and what to pursue in your own personal leadership development.

If you are a Christian, you do not have to worry whether the Bible applies to business. Your business is already working or failing based on whether it aligns or conflicts with the universal laws of existence. The more you understand what the Bible defines, the greater ability you have to see beyond the immediate.

Otherwise, you are far more myopic than you realize. The people who invested with Bernie Madoff appeared to be making great returns until everything crumbled. Granted, not all counterproductive approaches are that stark, nor fail that completely. Even Madoff was successful at covering up his fraudulent scheme for more than fifteen years. But productive long-term impact is only possible if it is based on what is true.

## The Ripple Effect

There are numerous (almost infinite) unintended consequences (ripple effects) from our decisions. We have significant logic ability, but everyone ultimately comes to the end of their capacity to fully comprehend the entirety of the environment in which they operate. The Bible is an absolute trustworthy source of authority that clarifies when we have come to the end of our understanding.

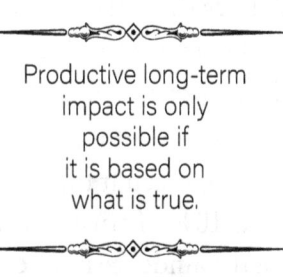

Productive long-term impact is only possible if it is based on what is true.

Some of the things the Bible commands are clear in their reason – but some are only partially clear, while some may only become clear centuries later or ultimately in eternity.

You can be confident God never commanded anything on a whim. Every principle or command is based on His infinite perspective of ultimate truth. As a result, each of them is universally beneficial.

Harmony with truth is productive. Disharmony with truth is destructive – always. You could say the Bible is the best "cheat sheet" for life because it gives you wisdom beyond your aptitude. It gives you ultimate success when you had no real understanding of the connection between your actions and end result. You can utterly depend on it.

## Choose

If you merely assume the Bible *applies* to business, you will begin with a question instead of full confidence. If the Bible merely applies, you are left with several questions: Does it actually apply to my situation? If so, how much? And if so, for me only, for my benefit only, or can others benefit as well?

But if you understand the Bible *subsumes* business – defines the categories and the laws by which business works best – your attitude and confidence create an exponentially different success rate.

As powerful as a reliable final source of authority is, if you approach it timidly, it loses most of its impact. It is the final 10% of trust that makes the most difference. Again, total confidence is necessary when choosing your final source of authority. You cannot be ambivalent or wishy-washy.

A biblical example of what this looks like is exemplified by Joshua. As the protégé of Moses, he was the leader who ultimately took the nation of Israel into the Promised Land. As he came to the end of his leadership of Israel, he was aware of the universal tendency to give incomplete and inadequate trust to what is your final source of authority. He knew the opportunities and challenges of what lay ahead of Israel were immense. Tentativeness would undermine their future. Total confidence would ignite them. So in Joshua 24:14, 15, here was his final challenge.

> 14 "Now fear the LORD and serve him with all faithfulness. Throw away the gods your ancestors worshiped beyond the Euphrates River and in Egypt, and serve the LORD. 15 But if serving the LORD seems undesirable to you, then choose for yourselves this day whom you will serve, whether the gods your ancestors served beyond the Euphrates, or the gods of the Amorites, in whose land you are living. But as for me and my household, we will serve the LORD."

If you want to read the whole challenge do a search on Joshua 24. You will find that Joshua was the precursor to the approach of many prolific coaches – productively confrontational. His bottom line – you are way too indecisive and spineless. If the going gets tough or you get distracted, you are going to wither, become fickle, and fade.

*As powerful as a reliable final source of authority is, if you approach it timidly, it loses most of its impact.*

If you wonder whether he was being too tough or negative, watch their response. Joshua's challenge ranks among the all-time best halftime coaching speeches. In response to his challenge – "choose today whom you will serve" – they made hard commitments that lasted for a generation.

Hear the core of Joshua's challenge:

> *"Choose"* – This speaks as much to what you won't do as to what you will do. To choose is to eliminate all other options.
>
> *"Today"* – Procrastinating is a productivity killer.
>
> *"Serve"* – You are making an all-out commitment. Give ultimate allegiance to your choice. Anything less is not fully a choice.

Viktor Frankl was an Austrian neurologist, psychiatrist, and founder of logotherapy. He is equally well known for his amazing story as a Holocaust survivor.

Here is an excerpt from an interview with Viktor Frankl in 1986, by Carole Charlewood, "the Oprah Winfrey of South Africa."

> *Carole:* Dr. Frankl, what is the difference between those who are able to pick themselves up, get over life's problems, and those who are not?
>
> *Dr. Frankl:* The decisive factor is decision – the freedom of choice, the freedom to come up with a decision. It should be, "I would like to become this way or another in spite of conditions that should only *seem* to fully determine my behavior. I wish to act freely as a responsible being... if need be in spite of the worst conditions." This is exactly what you could watch and witness under severe extreme

conditions of stress or tragic conditions.[6]

Your ability to choose well is what separates success from failure in the most intense circumstances. Being committed to an unwavering source of authority is essential. In that regard, the Bible is priceless.

What are the core values of your business? Where did they come from? On what are they based? Did you derive them from your personal tendencies, experiences, beliefs – or are they based on something greater, a source that transcends you?

# BELIEF TRANSFORMATION

## CHAPTER 5
Calibrate your beliefs:

- The Bible doesn't apply to business. It subsumes business. That is, it doesn't have to be adapted to work in business. It is defining why business works the way it does.

- The Bible isn't describing what it discovered to be true. It is clarifying what is true.

- Truths defined in the Bible are often reflected in the *best* leadership practices in business regardless of the religious beliefs of those businesses.

- The Bible is a declaration of what is true. As a result, it is an absolute, trustworthy filter and guide to what will work versus what will ultimately backfire.

- If you have complete confidence in your source of authority, you can follow its guidance even if the why is above your paygrade.

- Where we most need authoritative direction is where we are painfully clueless.

- The accuracy of our assumptions is often unrelated to the tenacity with which we hold them.

- When reality is counter to our intuition or heartfelt belief, we often will resist or even reject reality.

- Customer service done with a selfish motivation is merely customer manipulation.

- It is next to impossible to build a culture of customer service without understanding honor at the heart level.

- When the 10 Commandments call for honoring your father and mother, they are defining a fundamental principle that will determine the effectiveness of your business.

- Universal laws, like gravity, work regardless of your personal or stated corporate beliefs.

- The Bible is an absolutely trustworthy source of authority that clarifies when we have come to the end of our understanding.

- Harmony with what is true is productive. Disharmony with what is true is destructive – always.

- If you approach a final source of authority hesitantly, it loses most of its impact.

How do you know if concepts counter to your gut or the prevailing opinion are counterintuitive or just foolish?

How aware and confident are you in your final source of authority?

What role does what the Bible communicates play in your business? Why?

How aware are you of what you know and don't know?

What do you do to counter or support the areas that are above your paygrade but still affect your life and business?

# 6

## EXPERIENCE EXHILARATION:
### WHEN WHY YOU EXIST DEFINES WHAT YOU DO

"Cheshire Puss," she began, rather timidly, as she did not at all know whether it would like the name: however, it only grinned a little wider. "Come, it's pleased so far," thought Alice, and she went on, "Would you tell me, please, which way I ought to walk from here?"

"That depends a good deal on where you want to get to," said the Cat.

"I don't much care where——" said Alice.

"Then it doesn't matter which way you walk," said the Cat.

    - Lewis Carrol, Alice in Wonderland

We vaguely want a better life. But we are not completely sure what "a better life" is – as a result, we don't know how to get there.

What are you looking for from your job? What are you intending to produce, to create, to inspire? In addition, when it comes to your job, what would make you satisfied? Is a paycheck enough?

I have challenged many business leaders, "If you are living for the weekend, if you are living for retirement, you're missing the point." What you do in your "job" was never intended to merely make it possible for you to exist.

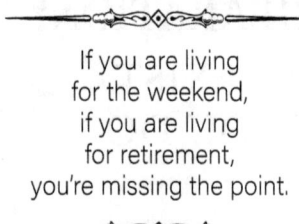

If you are living for the weekend, if you are living for retirement, you're missing the point.

Knowing this, Bill George, professor of management practice at Harvard Business School, researched what guides our business lives. In his book, *True North: Discover your Authentic Leadership*, he recounts an interview with Allen Horn, past president of Warner Brothers. Horn gave this description of the limitations of a paycheck.

> Early in your career, the incremental dollar can change the incremental quality of life because it enables you to buy a better car, a better house, etc. At some point however, the incremental dollar does not change the quality of life at all. In fact, incremental purchases just increase the complexity of life, not the enjoyment of life.[1]

In another of George's interviews, Alice Woodward put it this way:

> If you're just chasing the rabbit around the course, you're not running toward anything meaningful.[2]

Speaking of transformational leaders, John Maxwell said:

> They have a purpose, a why, that is bigger than they are. And that purpose literally compels them – allows them to blossom as a leader. It is the passion, the energy that allows them to be the person God has called them to be.

## Assessing What Inspires You

Consider an honest assessment of why you are in the job which currently provides your livelihood. How much of it is purposeful? Did you stumble into the position? Would you say your job basically happened to you or did you get there on purpose?

If any part of what got you to where you are was purposeful, what was the purpose? Even if your honest conclusion is that for the most part you just ended up in your job, is there anything about where you are that inspires you? Even if it is somewhat of a stretch to think that it inspires you, what benefit is there for your being there? You still are working at it, so there must be some kind of pull.

If you could do it all over again, what would you really want to do? How would you go about it? And most importantly, why?

Simon Sinek broke onto the business scene with his book, *Start with Why*. He defines what he calls The Golden Circle – which has three concentric circles. The outer circle is "What;" the middle circle is "How," and the inner circle is "Why." He reasons:

The Golden Circle provides compelling evidence of how much more we can achieve if we remind ourselves to start everything we do by first asking why.

The Golden Circle is an alternative perspective to existing assumptions about why some leaders and organizations have achieved such a disproportionate degree of influence.[3]

He continues,

"The goal is not to give you a course of action. The goal is to offer you the cause of action.[4]

You may or may not consider yourself an emotional person, but there is a cry inside all of us to live for a Why – a reason that is beyond ourselves. We may not understand the language or the source of the cry, but the evidence of it is everywhere. From inspiration to exasperation, from exhilaration to anxiety, the cry for a Why – for significance – reverberates through our life and through every culture.

In his exploration of Why, Sinek offers some great insights. We delve further by giving you clarity, plus the steps required in response to this cry.

## Three Levels of Internal Purpose

There are three potential levels of purpose for anything you do – Success, Significance, and Soul. Because words get used – even misused – to mean all kinds of things, I will briefly define what I mean by each of these.

By Success I mean the visible production of your life

— that part of life that is most easily quantifiable. It can be money made, a portfolio developed, a business or real estate acquired.

Significance is the tangible impact of your life. It may not be completely visible, but it often is still quite verifiable. It can include things like a life impacted or the quality of a culture or a business improved.

Soul is the inspired worship of your life. It is a level of purpose that is possible for anyone no matter what their belief system. It is not necessarily what you consciously worship but where you live out of the essential devotions of your life. It is the least tangible though oddly enough exponentially the most powerful.

## Success

Success is the most obvious, quantifiable, and immediately beneficial. Of the three levels it is the one that grabs our attention first. You could say it is the french fries and Coca-Cola in the meal of life. It is most readily managed and pays the fastest dividends. Some might be tempted to think this is the selfish level. Yet any level can be either self-focused or focused beyond yourself. This is either selfish or selfless – depending how you approach it.

People tend to look at Success as either the next savior or the next Satan. It really is neither. Instead, it just holds great value and great temptation – as do all of the levels. This level just happens to be the most accessible. The self-help industry does an incredible job of addressing Success. As a result, people tend to see the self-help industry from the same extremes as that of Success.

**S.M.A.R.T.** goals (Specific, Measureable, Achievable, Realistic, and Timely) focus on this level. No matter what level of purpose you achieve in life, this level should always retain value. That is important to understand, especially as we define the superior value of living out of the Significance and Soul levels.

> People tend to look at Success as either the next savior or the next Satan. It really is neither.

Ignore Success and you do it to your own demise. Even so, there is a sweet spot found outside of the extremes of ignoring or living for Success.[5]

## SIGNIFICANCE

In my mid-twenties when I was in graduate school, I discovered Bob Buford's book, *Half Time*. I shared the book with my father. He read it and thought it was a great book. But then asked this simple but intriguing question, "Why are you reading it?" I was beginning the first quarter of my business life – not half-time. Yet the thesis of the book grabbed me. Its challenge was to change your game plan from success to significance.

Buford describes the setting that brought him to discover a different way of looking at and living life. He writes:

> I have not always paid attention to my life. To be honest, I only began paying close attention when I reached my early forties and found myself in a success panic. I was

the president and CEO of a tremendously successful cable television company. I was fully engaged in a good and growing marriage. We had a son who was – there's no more appropriate way to say it – a prize.

And, of course, there was something gnawing at me. How was it that I could be so successful, so fortunate, and yet so frustratingly unfulfilled?[6]

In 2004, I joined a local Kiwanis club which was intent on making a difference. This group was made up of active business people with very positive attitudes on life. Together we built fantastic relationships, greatly expanded our understanding of the growing area northeast of Atlanta, and touched hundreds of lives. The difference we helped make was "one community, one child at a time."

While any organization has a degree of networking benefit, that was not our focus. Instead, we were focused on making a difference.

Many times I was struck by this group of business people who really didn't have time to do this (most of them ran their companies or their own businesses). Yet they had a passion for doing something of significance with their lives. The time and the money they spent making a difference would do little to help their businesses. But the improvements they made in others had a positive effect on them as well.

We have been designed for more than a paycheck. No matter what you do, where you live, or how you stack up on the food chain of corporate America or in the world economy as a whole – you want your life to have Significance.

Official titles may initially give you a voice. However, living at the Significance level of life is not determined by your economic success. True, you can leverage your Success. Because of that and other reasons Success will always have value. But you are not limited - neither do you get a pass in life – based on the visible production of your life.

## Soul

Sinek wrote in *Start with Why* about the power of charisma inspired by a Why. Here is his take on Bill Gates' success:*

> [Bill Gates] believes we can find ways to remove obstacles to ensure that everyone can live and work to their greatest potential.
>
> ... That belief inspired his vision of a PC on every desk to come to life. Ironic considering Microsoft never even made PCs. It wasn't just WHAT computers did that Gates saw the impact for the new technology, it was WHY we needed them. Today, the work he does with the Bill and Melinda Gates Foundation has nothing to do with software, but it is another way he has found to bring his WHY to life. He is looking for ways to solve problems. He still has an undying belief.
>
> ... For Gates, all that has changed is WHAT he is doing to bring his cause to life.[7]

Even though Bill Gates has an enormous financial tailwind to ignite what he is doing, what inspired him initially had to exist without that tailwind. His ongoing passion today indicates his inspiration was more than just Success.

---

*No attempt is made here or in future references to promote or speak to the vision of the Bill & Melinda Gates Foundation but rather to use their process to clarify some of the principles that can lead to greater effect.*

Even with all that Success could bring for Bill and Melinda Gates, they saw what to them was a life that has a potential beauty which eclipses mere Success.

Soul is the music of life.

Has it ever struck you that if you repeated a short talk at the same frequency you repeated a song you love, it would drive you and everyone around you crazy? Without getting too esoteric, there is something soulish about music. It can bring you to tears, create fear, inspire courage, and give peace even without words. Add words and it can take what is communicated to a transcendent level.

It is possible to live your life that way.

Indeed, it is more than just possible, for you were designed to live your life that way. This is evident in the fact that when we aren't living life this way, life feels empty or at least mildly unfulfilling. That's why we so easily live for the weekend and for retirement. If your life feels unfulfilling, the desire to escape increases.

Soul is the music of life.

It is interesting that the word "entertain" literally means to divert, amuse, or distract with something pleasant. If your job is unfulfilling, you instinctively develop an increasing desire to entertain yourself in some other way.

When your life loses its music, we call it burnout. Burnout is that pseudo-psychological term for how you feel when you lose sight of the reason you exist and find yourself chasing someone else's values, expectations, or *raison d'être*. Burnout seldom has anything to do with the amount of energy you are expending.

We instinctively sense that we were designed to do

something more than just exist. We were designed for someone or something greater than ourselves. Living out of Soul is discovering that thing or One and how we fit.

## The Discrepancy between the Sell and the Experience

On a few different occasions, I built construction businesses to help fund the initial development of our ministries as well as to help put myself through graduate school.

I once was coming home after a long day on the construction site. My stomach was on empty. Convinced I was starving, I stopped by a grocery store. At the time it seemed the best option to satisfy my ravishing hunger.

While browsing through the instant meal section, I came across a burrito meal which sounded appetizing. (Unfortunately, when you are starving almost anything looks good.)

With great anticipation I bought the meal, put it in the store's microwave, and dove in. Truth be told, I can eat about anything. My expectation was high; my stomach was poised; my mouth was watering in anticipation. In spite of everything I was anticipating, my newly acquired meal was about as savory as what I assume a mix of boiled socks and cardboard taste like.

I'm not sure how you can be that incompetent in making a burrito. I know it probably was not authentic Mexican, but how can you ruin a burrito? It's not rocket science. Someone had to work at being this bad. Despite every expectation of success and satisfaction, I was utterly disappointed.

Herein lies the challenge we face with any level of purpose:

we seldom know if experience will be commensurate with expectation until we have fully imbibed.

Success as the ultimate source of purpose is most attractive to those who have experienced it the least. The more you experience Success the less you believe in its ability to give ultimate satisfaction. Some people are more irrepressible in their belief in its ultimate value than others, but for most, the more they experience Success, the more they realize there has to be something greater. That was Bob Buford's experience.

I've never heard Bill Gates speak negatively of his experience of Success with Microsoft. Even so, don't overlook the fact that Bill and Melinda Gates are almost exclusively spending the second half of their lives in something that is not advancing the success of Microsoft. Instead they are creating Significance out of the Success he discovered through Microsoft.

You can choose to not believe me – and to ignore the experience of people like Bill Gates – and spend a substantial part of your life finding out the same thing for yourself. Or you can listen to the already nagging internal sense that Success has its limits and begin the process of reorienting yourself towards something greater.

## From a Job to a Calling

How would you describe what you do to generate income? What do you call what you do with the predominant part of your working day? Is it a job? A career?

A job is defined as "a piece of work… done for an agreed price" or "anything a person is expected or obliged to do;

duty; responsibility."[8]

The price part may be attractive, but aside from that the definition doesn't grab me as being very inspiring. There is real joy in producing something and the pride of a job well done. One of the innate satisfactions of building a business, or successfully fulling your role in a business, is being able to step back and see something actually being accomplished. Not all jobs having physical output, but inevitably the objective is for something to be constructed, achieved, or completed.

In addition, if your business is successful monetarily, you usually have the added benefit of increased options in life.

If you are goal motivated – seeing goals achieved, efforts being multiplied, positions, titles or degrees being conferred – these experiences are exciting and have real value. They are potent tools capable of being used for a greater good. What was just described is work at the Success level.

This is the action level of life. It is where most of us live. It is valuable. It is visible. And at a basic level it can be satisfying. Yet while the satisfaction may be immediate, it also is fleeting. There is always the sense of "OK, what's next?" Not resting on your laurels is a good thing – as long as you are not relying on the pursuit of Success for internal meaning.

This is ultimately why many jobs become known as "the rat race." Without something more, it just seems like an unending struggle with little ultimate meaning – like rats in pursuit of more cheese.

It has inspired many to change the way they look at their work – from seeing it as a job or even as a career to being

## EXPERIENCE EXHILARATION

awakened that there must be something more. They begin to desire to look beyond their immediate job, and instead to look ahead to what long-term impact they could make. How do I do more than just show up? How can what I do have significance beyond today? Rather than just working 9 to 5, what impact can I have on others?

Unfortunately most just double down in their pursuit of Success alone as they seek fulfillment. However, in a few cases frustration with the daily grind can become the catalyst for a change in focus. Instead of being totally captivated by Success, a few become more interested in pursuing Significance. It is not always clear what to do with the frustration, or even more positively, the growing urge to discover and commit to something more.

This book, *From Belief to Behavior*, and the coaching available through Beyond Sunday, Inc. are about taking you even further. These sources differentiate between what you will read in most other business or leadership books, conferences, or courses and what this book or an effective coach will provide.

Inevitably you will find even Significance has its limits. Significance has beauty in getting you beyond yourself – in making impact beyond yourself. One limit of Significance is the path it takes may or may not fully sync with who you were created to be.

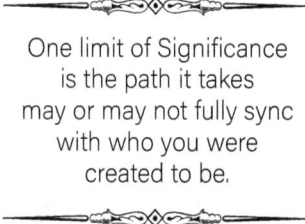

One limit of Significance is the path it takes may or may not fully sync with who you were created to be.

There are a lot of things you can do which will create Success. There are a lot of valuable organizations and individuals who are doing things of Significance. But why are you doing what you are doing? Did you just stumble on it? Did you happen to show up at the right time and the right place? Did a mix of your responsibilities, available opportunities, and limiting factors of life create a finite group of options, so you took what looked like the best one?

Are you aware that you are not just unique but were made unique for a specific purpose? Even though that's a statement of belief, it is accurate. The particular mix that defines you, as you, is not a mistake or a mere phenomenon of chance. You are every bit as specifically made as a contractor's tool or the program designed by a software engineer. And your uniqueness is even more valuable if you find it being used in a way that is apropos to your inherent design.

Do you know what it is like to sense you are in your sweet spot? There are few things like the feeling of a good fit between your intrinsic design and your actual life.

The idea of being called to what you do is often connected with the clergy. The truth is the same awareness of a calling is available to everyone. You can be so clearly designed for what you do and so internally drawn to what you do as to be called. In fact, anything less will leave you unfulfilled. Few things compare to the exhilaration of finding your fit.

There are few things like the feeling of a good fit between your intrisic design and your actual life.

An executive friend of mine with a Fortune 100 company shared one such experience where unique fit between ability and the specific requirements of the job became a game changer. To protect their reputations, I've changed the names of his company's suppliers to "A" and "B."

> In our procurement of one crucial piece of equipment for a major military contract, we only found two suppliers who could meet the customer's requirements.
> 
> "A" was already producing hundreds of units which, with just a few minor modifications, would fully satisfy the customer's requirements. By contrast, "B" was developing a sensor they claimed would meet the required specifications – but their new project was just a "paper tiger."
>
> Based on their lower risk and lower development cost, "A" won the initial competition. But before informing either firm of our selection, we first had to get the customer's concurrence.
>
> "A's" product was already flying in another military application. But the official who had to approve our selection totally surprised us. He rejected our decision! He then gave us this very foolish but explicit reason: "I don't want a piece of junk from another military service on our program!" But "A's" product definitely was not "junk." It already had proved its capabilities in the "real world."
>
> His rejection of our selection became irreversible, however, when at his direction the customer issued a new "spec" which only "B" could meet. We had no other option: "B" won the contract.
>
> We immediately scheduled a review of how "B" planned to provide us an initial unit in the limited six month window. In this review we learned that to satisfy the tight aircraft dimensions, "B" would have to develop a

brand new chip to replace the much larger circuitry in their development model.

During lunch I asked their chief engineer how "B" was ever going to deliver this new integrated circuit chip in just six months. The engineer grabbed a napkin off the lunch table and drew the following diagram with his pen:

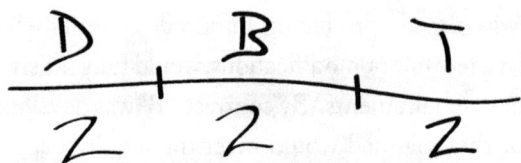

I said, "Let me guess: D,B,T means Design, Build, Test and 2,2,2 is how you get to six months." He shook his head.

I told him his "back of the napkin" diagram was "nuts." No one had ever developed such a complex chip in six months. And D, B, T showed a total lack of thought or understanding of the process. Despite the risk, the customer had insisted that we select this "paper tiger" design – but it placed our schedule commitment in serious jeopardy.

I therefore told company B they had to develop a new plan. We would meet again in a few weeks to evaluate their revised plan. A few weeks later, to my amazement, "B" presented us with a large PERT chart. It showed, in great detail, exactly how they would confidently meet our need for a unit to use in our integration lab in just six months.

Their PERT chart contained every task "B" had to complete. It also had a more realistic eleven-month cycle for chip development, but with a very adequate temporary work-around. "B" would supply a unit for our integration lab in six months. But because a lab unit didn't need to meet the aircraft size requirements, "B" could use the larger circuitry of their development unit while they still developed the chip needed for the much tighter dimensions of the units to be used in the aircraft.

I couldn't comprehend how "B" had gone, in such a short time, from a totally nonsensical "back of the napkin" idea to a very detailed PERT chart which reflected every required task. So I asked.

They had hired a subcontractor who specialized in developing highly credible, detailed PERT charts. These PERT experts so impressed me that we hired the same experts ourselves to help us schedule our own programs. Years later, when this subcontractor decided to close the office nearest to us, we got their permission to hire some of their best people from this local operation.

As my executive friend shared his experience, it struck me again of the power of a close fit between someone's "calling" and the focus of their job. People who truly enjoyed analyzing and graphing internal processes allowed company B to go from being a schedule disaster to having total insight into the challenges which lay ahead of them.

Experts from the same subcontractor were then able to provide identical benefits to my friend's much larger and more complex company – significantly expanding the analysists' impact and careers.

Truly, these people saw what they did as more than just

"a job." They actually enjoyed learning the exact details of how a company saw their development process – and then providing the necessary insight into the "nitty-gritty" of this process to develop a very detailed PERT schedule which overcame every difficulty while still meeting the necessary development schedule. Because of their love for this kind of challenge, they provided the same highly productive insight time and time again.

## Business Confidence – Finding Your Value

We all want to believe we have value. The appeal of Significance is that it provides a greater sense of value. But if your value is determined by the success of what you do, you are always at risk of losing your sense of value.

Confidence comes from understanding that your innate value is not defined by what you do. Your value predated anything you have ever done since it is connected to the purpose for which you were created. This discovery produces an unequaled release and freedom.

One of the greatest sources of stress is the attempt to attain value through what you do, or what you have, or how people perceive you. Eliminate those sources of stress, and your anxiety level drops drastically.

The only way to release that false yardstick of value is to realize you don't have to do something Successful in order to become valuable. In fact you don't have to do something Significant either. *This doesn't eliminate the importance of Success or Significance; it merely redefines their place and purpose.*

There is an innate need to have value. Stop and consider

why bullying is such a major issue in our culture today.

The predominant issue is not one kid punching another. It is publicly devaluing someone, whether in person or via cyberspace. The felt issue is very real as demonstrated by the fact that people have committed suicide as a result of bullying.

Whether you have ever struggled with bullying as a child, the same challenge affects every adult. If the source of your value is misdirected, you will experience anxiety. By establishing the basis for your value accurately and productively, you will create confidence and emotional stability which will serve you well.

This is what Herb Cohen referred to regarding his ability to accurately assess the Iran hostage crisis. As previously cited, his response to people's amazement at his accuracy of discernment was that, "I didn't have a career or reputation invested in the crisis. And I was less inhibited by a desire for acceptance or fear of disapproval."

Clearly the basis for Cohen's sense of value did not ride on a "desire for acceptance or fear of disapproval."

## Soul Calling and Value

The beauty of living life out of the Soul level is it begins with the realization that you already have been designed. It doesn't require you to achieve or create something.

The challenge of Kurt Goldstein and Abraham Maslow's "self-actualization" is to realize your potential – everything you are capable of becoming. Their discoveries came from observing people. What this book communicates comes initially from observing a biblical source.

Independent of the source, there is relatively universal evidence that people instinctively realize they were created with a unique purpose.

If you realize this inherent value is woven into you and that you don't need to create or conjure up this value – in fact, if you recognize that you can neither create this value nor can it be taken from you – these realizations have an amazing impact.

There is intense benefit of being in pursuit of the God who created you. Having said that, in His words, He causes it to "rain on the just and the unjust." That is - the laws of harvest, economy, psychology, and all the other "natural" laws He designed work no matter what your belief system is.

Whether you consider yourself a person of faith or not, living life out of the Soul level is the most powerful way to live. Rather than merely producing a product or creating an impression, living at the Soul level gives real and satisfying purpose to life. It is living life for a purpose not merely a product.

This is what Simon Sinek refers to as "Starting with Why." The lack of this perspective fatally undermined Ken Lay's life and career. The presence of this perspective ignited David Livingstone. And it is reflected in the ability of Herb Cohen – whenever he approaches Success and Significance – to "care… but not that much." Living at the Soul level allowed Bill Gates to seamlessly transition from leading Microsoft to leading the Gates Foundation, even though the two organizations have totally different objectives.

With such power, impact, and universal availability, it

may seem shocking that more people don't live this way. A primary reason they don't is because living out of Soul requires great risk - a risk we examine in chapter 7.

# BELIEF TRANSFORMATION

## CHAPTER 6
Calibrate your beliefs:

- If you are living for the weekend, if you are living for retirement, you're missing the point.

- Transformational leaders have a purpose, a why, that is bigger than they are.

The following words are specifically defined, and so they are capitalized throughout the book to distinguish them from the general use of the same terms:

- *Success* is the visible product of your life. It is most easily quantifiable.

- *Significance* is the tangible impact of your life. Not always fully visible – like the influence a person has on others – but it is often still verifiable.

- *Soul* is the inspired worship of your life. It is where you live out of the fundamental devotion of your life. It is the least tangible but the most powerful.

- *Success* is readily managed and pays the fastest dividends. It is the focus of most S.M.A.R.T. goals.

- We have been designed for more than a paycheck. No matter what you do, you want your life to have *Significance*.

- *Soul* is the music of life.
- If your life feels unfulfilling, the desire to escape increases.
- Burnout is when you lose sight of the reason you exist. It seldom is sparked by the amount of energy you are expending.
- Living out of Soul is discovering the main thing or the One and how we fit.
- Success as the ultimate source of purpose is most attractive to those who have experienced it the least.
- There are few things like the feeling of a good fit between your intrinsic design and your actual life.
- If your value is determined by the success of what you do, you are always at risk of losing your sense of value.
- Confidence comes from understanding your value is innate and not defined by what you do.
- If the source of your value is misdirected, you will experience anxiety.

What are you looking for from your job, from life?

What would make you satisfied or fulfilled?

How did you arrive at your present job setting? Choice, opportunity, just happened, purposeful process?

How you would describe your present vocation - a job, a career, or a calling? Do you feel called to or designed for what you do?

How would you define your Soul design, your reason for being?

# 7

# LEVERAGE YOUR LIFE:
## COMMIT TO ESSENTIAL RISK

This is the true joy in life, the being used for a purpose recognized by yourself as a mighty one; the being thoroughly worn out before you are thrown on the scrap heap; the being a force of Nature instead of a feverish selfish little clod of ailments and grievances complaining that the world will not devote itself to making you happy. And also the only real tragedy in life is the being used by personally minded men for purposes which you recognize to be base.[1]
 - George Bernard Shaw

You have a choice. Your life can be a life based on a purpose specific to and yet greater than you. Or your life can be a mere to-do list of things that need to be done – items to be checked off as they're completed.

Ever wonder what makes amusement and entertainment

so attractive? The to-do list approach sends us looking for seasoning on a life that would otherwise feel dull. Amusement is a sugar addiction intended to distract from the sense of the meaninglessness of a hollow purpose. Interestingly amusement literally means to divert or distract.

But when the to-do lists of life are in pursuit of something greater, they take on greater value. To-do lists are like tofu. They take on the taste of whatever they are around. They are something to sink your teeth into. But left to themselves they are tasteless.

As a result, many have discovered the need to focus their to-do lists into a fine laser and point them toward a worthwhile goal. This creates a serious challenge. Does the goal on which they are focused have inherent value, or is it just a bigger piece of tofu?

You have things you are going to do today. You may not label them as such, but they are your to-do lists. To-do lists are simply very specific, immediate, and attainable goals. They are the building blocks and prerequisites to larger goals. But are your larger goals worthy? Or are they just big to-do lists – significant achievements, impressive when written down on a score card, but without real significance at the Soul level?

The movie, *The Guardian*, tells of the Aviation Survival Technician program – the U.S. Coast Guard's "A" school that trains their rescue swimmers to navigate in the most extreme conditions. Ashton Kutcher plays Jake Fischer (dubbed "Goldfish") – a high school swimming champion who is selfish, undisciplined, and extremely talented.

Senior Chief, Ben Randall, played by Kevin Costner,

confronts the recruits one day:

> Today we were going to learn about how to approach a drowning victim in high seas. But I think there are some here that aren't interested in that victim. In fact, I think there are some here in this class that aren't interested in saving lives at all. I believe there are some who are more interested in setting records. So today is record day.

Undaunted, Goldfish sets out on a tear to break every record on the board. Surprisingly the Senior Chief begins exuding accolades in Goldfish's direction such as: "Wow, he is fast." "He's good." "You people do not deserve to be in the same pool as Jake – he's destroying you."

But the longer the day goes on the more it becomes clear the grandiose statements are actually intended to put a question mark on the value of merely beating a record. The real records are the lives saved or lives lost.

## The Limits of Success

There is true beauty to Success, and that beauty should never become obsolete. I am not convinced there is any benefit to demeaning the value of Success, and I have no desire to do so.

The personal development industry often does a masterful job of expanding people's skill in successfully achieving their goals. However the beauty of Success can quickly become hollow. This leads to a love-hate relationship with Success – due both to its power and its limitations.

The external effect of what we accomplish (the visible production of our life) has enormous value. Most everything that allows you to make impact is because someone was successful at something. Unless you are a hermit who lives entirely off the land with no assistance from any tools, you are continuously benefiting from someone's success.

Herein is the key. The true value of Success lies with how it is affecting others and a purpose beyond ourselves. If you honestly reflect it quickly becomes clear, there must be – there needs to be – something beyond Success.

The initial attractiveness of Success comes from our ability to measure it. It is the quantifiable aspect of purpose. It is the most visible and therefore the most immediately effectible and affecting. It creates the most instant gratification.

Instant gratification has developed a negative connotation. But it is not inherently negative – unless it becomes the driving force. This is the intrinsic limitation of Success. It is great as a tool and as a means of evaluation – but terrible as one's primary motivation or ultimate purpose. It is like trying to date a robot – it is meaningless for its own sake.

A directly consumable aspect of Success is money. It is called a liquid asset because of its ease of use. It creates clear and immediate effect. In my experience few believe they are controlled by money, but it is amazing how a little of it will motivate people to do a lot of things.

All of these factors illustrate why Success has a tendency to become people's primary objective.

## Success Attachment

How attached are you to your present situation? To your present success?

If your ship came in would you be ready?

How about if another opportunity arose with a lot of potential to improve your financial situation, how willing would you be to jump on that ship?

People and businesses often are not completely clear on their Why. As a result, they may not know how to distinguish between a real opportunity and a nice look-a-like.

Even if you have a relatively clear understanding of where you want to go, how committed are you to that vision? How willing are you to venture what you already have in order to achieve what you could become?

To continue the earlier metaphor, if you have a relatively good ship now, how difficult would it be to get off that ship in order to board a more productive ship?

We all love to live vicariously through the successes of others. Sports fans do it all the time. Whether it is sports, business, relationships, lifestyles, or any other image of success, we love fantasizing about how exciting it would be to be in someone else's place.

What we often ignore is what it took for those we idolize to get where they are.

## An Ultimate Example

Earlier I challenged you that the Bible does not apply to business; it subsumes business. The Bible defines the most fundamental laws of existence – the fabric of everything. This includes why your business is a success, a catastrophe, or somewhere in between.

The most powerful example of the Bible defining the laws of existence is seen in the historical crux of the reason for the Bible.

If you have been exposed to even the basics of Christianity, you know that Jesus came as a baby, grew up, and was ultimately put to death via crucifixion – a torturous version of capital punishment perfected by the Romans.

What many are not aware of is how enormously successful Jesus was prior to his crucifixion.

You may have heard of him miraculously feeding 5,000 and then later 4,000 people from just a few loaves and fish. The Bible actually indicates the number with this annotation – "not counting women and children." (Matthew 14:21; 15:38) Considering how many children a family would have, he easily was regularly impacting 20,000+ people. In his travels across Palestine, huge crowds came out from the local towns and villages to hear him speak.

The crowds continued to grow. Just prior to his crucifixion, his fame was mushrooming. Seeing the massive crowds following Jesus, the religious elites and power brokers of the day became desperate in their attempts to defeat him – to the point of plotting means to assassinate him. They looked at the huge crowds and had this assessment of their attempts to stop him, "See, this is getting us nowhere. Look how the whole world has gone after him!" (John 12:19).

The Pharisees said this as the people streamed into Jerusalem for the Passover. Upwards of 2 to 3 million people would have been present. This in a day prior to planes, trains, and automobiles. On everyone's mind was one thing – see Jesus. They lined the streets coming into Jerusalem just to get a glimpse of him.

They basically mulched the road and threw blankets in the path just so the donkey Jesus was riding would have a smooth path – a type of rolling out of the red carpet. They waved palm branches as if to welcome a king. In fact, many were crying out for him to be king.

> What many are not aware of is how enormously successful Jesus was prior to his crucifixion.

Yet these millions were a mere drop in the bucket in comparison to the ultimate impact he came to make. Jesus, of all people, understood how precarious success can be. He understood timing like no one before or after him.

As it is often said, timing is everything. We take that to mean if you have a good thing going grab on – "strike while the iron is hot," or numerous other sayings about making your move when you have the chance.

As Jesus' fame swelled, he began showing a completely different approach. He began sharing it with those closest to him, his disciples. What he revealed to them wasn't a transient paradigm shift but a veritable explosion of their entire worldview.

Jesus gave them this insight into the next step: "I die."

What?!?

Indeed, that's exactly how his disciples responded. "What?"

As a leader among the twelve disciples, Peter was often the most willing to stick his neck out. Peter essentially told Jesus, "Over my dead body" – or a little closer paraphrase, "That's never going to happen, and if necessary I'll die to make sure it doesn't."

Before you jump to conclusions, understand Jesus didn't have a martyr complex. In fact, he didn't have a messiah *complex*. He had a messianic *calling*. He literally was the Messiah. It was why he was born. He didn't come to be a king. He came to be the Savior.

Being a king and returning Israel to the gilded age it once enjoyed would have been amazing. Who knows how that would have played out in the history books. But that wasn't his purpose.

Your perception of Jesus may skew your understanding of how challenging this decision was. When Matthew and Luke speak of Jesus being tempted in the wilderness prior to the beginning of his public ministry, it was real temptation. They relate how Satan tempted Jesus.

One temptation was for Jesus to use his power to supernaturally make bread out of stones – give himself an "unfair" advantage over everyone else in getting through life – Chick-fil-A without standing in line. He hadn't eaten for 40 days. The word they used indicated he was seriously hungry, and he was nowhere near food.

Satan also tempted him by showing him the kingdoms of the world and challenging him that Satan could give them to Jesus for free – an easier way out, no cross required. Even at the very end just prior to crucifixion, Jesus was begging his Father – if there was another way, he wanted it.

When Peter did the "over my dead body" reaction, Jesus' response to Peter was, "Get behind me, Satan! You are a stumbling block to me." Or in other words, "Get out of here. You are seriously creating a destructive temptation for me."

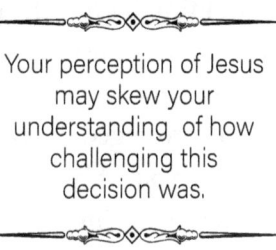
Your perception of Jesus may skew your understanding of how challenging this decision was.

The temptation to avoid risk and stop at Success was real. He could have taken the immediate Success and run with it. The world was coming to him. It was tempting. But he held Success loosely, and he leveraged it for something infinitely greater.

So in Matthew 16:24-26 it relates how he responded to Peter and the rest of the disciples who were in shock:

> 24 Then Jesus said to his disciples, "Whoever wants to be my disciple must deny themselves and take up their cross and follow me. 25 For whoever wants to save their life will lose it, but whoever loses their life for me will find it. 26 What good will it be for someone to gain the whole world, yet forfeit their soul? Or what can anyone give in exchange for their soul?

Why does this matter to you and your business? You aren't Jesus. You are definitely not the Savior. Aside from a religious lesson, why have I related this?

The attitude, approach, and decisions of Jesus indicate an incredible business lesson. It has the potential of changing everything about the why and the way you do business – and this includes your effectiveness and success.

First, as we discover what this defines about life and

business, the first consideration is how much your belief matters. In fact, as highest importance, what you believe about Him matters the most. The most important question you will ever answer is what will you do with the offer of Jesus to you.

He leveraged everything for you. More specifically, he died for you. His intent is to radically and permanently renovate your life. For his leverage to be effective in your life – His only requirement: recognize you need forgiveness and his right to forgive you, and give him ultimate authority based on absolute trust. In response to your honesty and trust toward him, he will enable you to love him and to love others like he does.

His leverage can become the ground off of which you leverage. His leverage offers a life-changing proposition – one that is worthy of your focus and time. Beyond Sunday, the organization I lead, exists to help leaders work out this opportunity.

Beyond that, the incredible principles wrapped up in the account I just related directly apply to your business. Jesus' mission was unique. No one has or will ever repeat it. However, the way he went about it is one of the most powerful business lessons you can learn.

Jesus lived out, at the ultimate level, what can best be described as "Leverage."

Whether it is Bob Buford, Kiwanians, Bill Gates, or anyone else who has discovered purpose beyond success, how do you move from Success to Significance to Soul? If living out of Soul is so much better – if living from a sense of calling rather than just a need to succeed makes such a difference – how do you get there?

There are three steps for initiating the process of moving from Success to Soul – of leveraging the good to achieve the truly great.

## Step One - Clarify Your Design, Motives, and Purpose

Both Jesus and the religious elite had a passion and purpose to transform the beliefs of the people of Israel. However, their underlying motives and objectives were drastically different.

Design, motives, and purpose are not the same. It's helpful to the point of astounding when they are working in tandem, but even then they are distinct.

Design is inherent. Design is always created for a purpose, but you can choose a purpose other than one that relates to your design. Motives are the inspiration that ignite how you actively use your design for the purpose you intend.

Motivation involves inspiration. It is a catalyst to action. As with character, motivations are effectible but operate predominantly by default – arising out of your worldview. Motivations are easily hidden, distorted, even conflicting. They are the most simplistic level of value and belief. They are powerful forces and when harnessed well can be "the wind beneath your wings."

Purpose speaks to the ultimate aim. While purpose can be very motivating, it speaks more specifically to the goal of the motivation. You have the ability to choose the purpose you pursue. And it is when that purpose concurs with your deepest – and inherent – design that purpose rises to the pinnacle of its effectiveness.

The value and impact of purpose matching design is core to the economy of life. This is seen at a basic level in tools. Take, for example, a simple screwdriver.

A screwdriver can be used for a lot of purposes other than its intended design: as a pry bar, chisel, its handle as a hammer, a stirrer, or to extract the pin from a door hinge. While it can work in a pinch for a lot of purposes, using it "in a pinch" often leads to at least low-grade frustration: it bends as a pry bar, dulls or is too small as a chisel, smashes your hand when it slips off the nail you pounded, is paint covered from the last stirring, and is too wide to dislodge the hinge pin.

It is most effective when used as a screwdriver with an appropriately sized screw. In fact, few things can replace the effectiveness of a screwdriver for fastening something with a screw.

That may be a simple example, but it accurately reflects the power of your chosen purpose matching your design. It also illustrates why we need to clarify – and possibly modify – our fundamental motivations before attempting to achieve our objectives.

What inspires you? What presently has your attention? What gets you up in the morning or gets you down during the day? Take a look at your calendar. Take a look at your checkbook or credit card statement. What do the entries indicate?

Earlier we stated that our actions are expressions of our beliefs. If we were fully balanced, holistic and mature people, our actions would instinctively implement our purposes.

Following belief with actions would be natural – have a belief… live out an action… complete our objective. But such consistency requires a belief system, or worldview, which matches our conscious purposes. Our objectives will be completed harmoniously only when our actions – which reflect what we actually believe at a Soul level – parallel what we claim we want to see take place.

The challenge is initially we aren't that holistically balanced. We have all kinds of internal beliefs. Some are productive; some are destructive. Some are settled; some are transient. Some are clear; some are vague or even confused. Inopportunely, many are even competing.

We need to get a better grasp on our values and beliefs. Our values and beliefs inevitably affect our motivation which then result in our actions. Motivations are the easiest entry point to discovering the connection between our beliefs and actions. Conversely, pursuing a greater purpose without clarifying our motivations is like trying to walk a straight line in the midst of a hurricane – remotely possible but frustrating.

If we can evaluate the actual motives which result in the actions we take, such an assessment can provide a readily accessible yardstick of our actual worldview. In the process of discovering your true motivations, one of the first things you will realize is that some of your beliefs may actually be competing – especially if they are conflicting.

> Pursuing a greater purpose without clarifying our motivations is like trying to walk a straight line in a hurricane - remotely possible but frustrating.

Getting a handle on your motivations is critical. In order to harness the winds of motivation, you have to understand which way they are blowing.

Once you get a handle on your motivations, you are ready for the second step.

## Step Two - Realize Everything is a Tradeoff

Atlanta traffic is known for having insane commute times. Thirty minutes each way is considered good. I have a friend who discovered a "great" way to redeem that time: read a book. I'm not talking about audio books on CD or via Bluetooth. I'm speaking of actually reading a book while driving. Considering his actions, I probably need to add the medical disclaimer to the inside cover, "Don't drive or operate heavy machinery while reading this book."

My friend's actions are a puerile example of the problem, and foolishness, of not accepting the fact that everything is a tradeoff.

Any choice you make is as much a choice of what you will not do as what you will do. You chose to read this book, so I'm assuming you are not driving or doing much of anything else for the moment. You choose to go to work which means for that time you will not be with your family.

But what about the multitaskers among us?

They don't exist!

Travis Bradberry writes in *Forbes* magazine:

> Research conducted at Stanford University found that multitasking is less productive than doing a single thing

at a time. The researchers also found that people who are regularly bombarded with several streams of electronic information cannot pay attention, recall information, or switch from one job to another as well as those who complete one task at a time.

But what if some people have a special gift for multitasking? The Stanford researchers compared groups of people based on their tendency to multitask and their belief that it helps their performance. They found that heavy multitaskers—those who multitask a lot and feel that it boosts their performance—were actually worse at multitasking than those who like to do a single thing at a time. The frequent multitaskers performed worse because they had more trouble organizing their thoughts and filtering out irrelevant information, and they were slower at switching from one task to another. Ouch.

Multitasking reduces your efficiency and performance because your brain can only focus on one thing at a time. When you try to do two things at once, your brain lacks the capacity to perform both tasks successfully.[2]

The Stanford study cited in this *Forbes* article indicates that multitasking actually produces an inability to stay on task, to stay focused. Multitasking is actively breaking down the boundaries that define your focus. In their words, it makes people "suckers for irrelevancy."[3]

Tradeoffs are the price we pay for everything we do. Ignoring the price of tradeoffs is like spending with a credit card and ignoring the bill. The concept of tradeoffs has been used to help people get a grip on their personal spending habits.

The proposition is since it takes time to make money, consider your purchases in relationship to how much of your life you are giving up. How long does it take me to make this much spendable money? Based on that, this new TV is costing a certain amount of hours or days of my life. Is the time it takes me to earn that much money worth spending on a larger TV?

At first the idea of tradeoffs feels negative and restrictive. However, when done well, it is actually freeing. Not only does trading off well increase the productivity of your life, it gives you the freedom to live fully in the moment – to live undistracted.

When I think through tradeoffs well, I prepare in advance well. When I prepare in advance well, I schedule times to do the things that need to be done. When I schedule things that need to be done, it gives me the freedom to do what is presently on my schedule. Other things that are pressing and that would otherwise distract my attention can be set aside for the time being. I don't have to worry about the other things that also need to be done. Those things have their day and time in my schedule, but not now.

Understanding tradeoffs helps you to *proactively* make those necessary decisions that you otherwise would make *reactively*. You are not God. You are not omnipresent, omniscient, or omni-anything. Since you are human, tradeoffs are not merely the right thing to do. They are what happens.

Victoria Azarenka, former World #1 in women's tennis, made this comment about her developmental years. "I was missing out on a lot of things that my friends were doing, but in another way, they were missing things I was doing. It was kind of a tradeoff I had to make."

Whether or not you set your priorities through conscious tradeoffs, "reality bites" anyhow. When reality bites, things happen to you rather than being managed by necessary tradeoffs.

The disciples who joined Jesus early on in his ministry were highly passionate. Unlike Jesus they were also clueless about the extent of the tradeoffs being a disciple would require. They made some initial tradeoffs – leaving their businesses for example. But that was just the first installment. History indicates every one of them, except John, ended up paying with their lives. Even John spent the end of his life in exile on the bleak Island of Patmos.

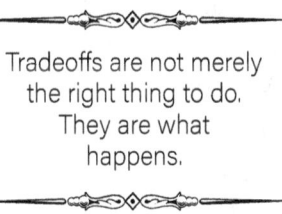

Tradeoffs are not merely the right thing to do. They are what happens.

One of the top barriers to business development I see is an ignorance of the tradeoffs required to succeed. This is equally true when it comes to living your life at the highest level – the Soul level. Recognizing and embracing the tradeoffs is the price of admission.

Prepare; choose wisely; choose in advance, and you get ahead of the tradeoff curve – you ride the wave. Ignore this reality; react in the moment, and you get crushed by the unavoidable waves of resulting tradeoffs life sends you.

An inane and problematic tendency we have is we prefer being forced to make tradeoffs rather than having to choose them. Painful tradeoffs I can no longer avoid seem more palatable than the elected pain of tradeoffs I have purposefully chosen. Our frequent failure to recognize this tendency doesn't reduce the accuracy of this diagnosis.

The difficulty of making hard choices is a turnoff. Yet, when we continue to say yes to multiple opportunities because they are attractive, intriguing, or just hard to say no to - living with diminished effectiveness becomes the frustrating reality of our attempts to multitask.

One of the greatest hindrances to moving from Success to Soul is Success itself. Success becomes our greatest enemy when it keeps us stuck – attached to our present existence. What got you to where you are seldom can get you to where you need to go. John Maxwell put it this way, "You've got to give up to go up."[4]

The more effective you are at developing, the greater this challenge becomes. Initially, good tradeoffs often involve just eliminating the negative things from our lives. The longer you practice the discipline of tradeoffs, however, the more it requires eliminating even good things in order to focus on what is not just good, but actually the best.

This leads to the final lynchpin.

## Step Three - Commit to Leverage as the Ultimate Tradeoff

Whether you consider yourself a great success or not, being willing to put real or potential success at risk takes incredible commitment and courage.

Every parent ultimately faces the challenge of releasing their children. It is why parents raise their children – so that their children can live life as they were designed.

Ironically, while every parent believes they raise their

children to be productive adults, releasing them to adulthood is always a challenge. Once children get farther and farther away from the authority of the home, the direct control of their parents drops off dramatically.

This challenge has personally become very real to me as my own daughters transition into their twenties. I know my maturity is greater than that of my girls. It had better be – I've had decades more experience and development than they have. But if they are to become fully effective adults, I cannot keep making decisions for them.

Releasing is a very real risk. Releasing is risking that the character, values, and beliefs you tried to instill in them will stick. Releasing is risking that the maturity instilled will be sufficient to counterbalance the necessary maturity they have yet to obtain. Releasing is the legitimate and right risk of taking your hands off so that the character you intended to develop in them can have its effect.

Parenting requires everything you have – physically, emotionally, and financially. This means when you release them, you are risking all of that investment to someone far less mature than you – someone who may have a very different perspective than yours.

But parents cannot continue to maintain authority in the lives of their children if they sincerely want them to develop into full maturity. Maturity by essence equates to taking responsibility, and authority should always be commensurate with responsibility. Therefore, a parent must release authority into their child's control at the same rate they seek for maturity to take root in their child.

The process starts years before they go fully on their

own – simple things like choosing their own clothes in the morning or which foods they will eat at meal time. How those are traded off against parental authority is a challenge that each parent must face. Tradeoff before they are ready and you don't instill fully the character and values you desire. Hold on too tightly and the values you want to instill don't have the opportunity to take root.

When a tradeoff is executed well, greater risk results in greater impact.

Jesus implicitly understood the reality of tradeoffs. He wasn't trying to impress people with his selflessness. While his life is the supreme example, his primary goal was not merely to create a moral tale for the benefit of the listeners. He lived out the ultimate tradeoff. As he did it, he challenged those following him to make tradeoffs which seemed just as extreme as his own.

The life of Jesus is a perfect, quantifiable example of the power of leverage.

Just as he challenged, a core aspect of leverage is: to win in life you have to be willing to lose your life. This is not simply about being moral. It is not just the good thing to do; it is how life works. This is what it takes to win ultimately.

To be succinct about what Jesus leveraged: He leveraged the prerogatives of being God and became human (Philippians 2:5-11); he leveraged the opportunity to be king (John 6:15); he leveraged his right to be honored (Isaiah 53); he leveraged the overwhelming success he had at the beginning; he even uniquely leveraged the Soul level of his life (2 Corinthians 5:21; Matthew 27:46). Having paid an extraordinary price and having been successful at accomplishing everything he came to do, he then leveraged his success all over again by turning it over to a small group of his core leaders.

Fundamentally, leverage is a transfer of force, of power. And it always involves risk. It is the tradeoff of risking the safety of what I have in order to obtain what I desire to achieve. Real leverage involves real potential for loss.

Sometimes leverage requires a certainty of loss. For Jesus, he understood it was ultimately going to cost him his life. But risk does not always equal loss. Rather, it is the *willingness* to lose something in order to gain something greater.

It has been said that the most dangerous person is someone who has nothing to lose. A more accurate statement is that it is someone who is *willing* to lose everything he may have.

To be willing to lose everything in order to attain your greatest purpose is like eliminating the governor from the engine of your life. The intense effect is so universal that it even can be manipulated for destructive purposes in the sense of a suicide bomber. But harnessing absolute leverage to your purpose creates intense, rewarding results.

On Thursday, April 4, 1968 at the Lorraine Motel in Memphis Tennessee, Martin Luther King, Jr. lost his life in pursuit of a dream. He wasn't the only one fighting for civil liberties, but he became its primary icon and tipping point in the modern era.

The day before his assassination, as he concluded his final speech, these were his words:

Like anybody, I would like to live a long life. Longevity has its place. But I'm not concerned about that now. I just want to do God's will. And He's allowed me to go up to the mountain. And I've looked over. And I've seen the Promised Land. I may not get there with you. But I want you to know tonight, that we, as a people, will get to the Promised Land!

That is a statement of leverage – the ultimate tradeoff. What do you need to leverage? What is enjoyable, yet unnecessary to get where you need to go? What is valuable, yet not as valuable as your ultimate purpose?

# BELIEF TRANSFORMATION

## Chapter 7
Calibrate your beliefs:

- Apart from sufficient purpose, entertainment becomes a way of distracting ourselves from the lack of meaningfulness in life – a coping mechanism.

- Success can be highly valuable, even beautiful. Yet without a greater purpose as its target, it becomes meaningless.

- The most powerful life in history, that of Jesus, is an absolute roadmap of what it means to live out of Soul by leveraging your life – leverage the good to achieve the great.

- *Step One:* Clarify your design, motives, and purpose.

- Design is inherent, built in.

- Motivation involves inspiration. It is a catalyst for action.

- Real motivation is deeper than emotion and arises out of our worldview.

- Purpose speaks to ultimate aim, the goal of motivation, the reason for design.

- Purpose is most powerful when it is in sync with design.

- If we were fully balanced, holistic and mature people, our actions would instinctively implement our purposes. The overwhelming tendency is to not be that holistically aligned.

- *Step Two:* Realize everything is a tradeoff.

- Productive multitasking is a fantasy.

- Tradeoffs are the price we pay for everything we do. Ignoring the price of tradeoffs is like spending with a credit card and ignoring the bill.

- Understanding tradeoffs leads to better preparation, reduced stress, greater freedom, and amplified output.

- Embrace tradeoffs, and you ride the wave they produce. Ignore tradeoffs, and you get crushed by the inevitable waves of default tradeoffs that follow.

- *Step Three:* Commit to leverage as the ultimate tradeoff.

- When a tradeoff is executed well, greater risk results in greater impact.

- To win in life, you have to be willing to lose your life.

- Leverage is risking the safety of what I have in order to obtain what I desire to achieve.

How attached are you to your present pursuits or vocation?

Have you written out your design, purpose, mission, vision, or core values?

Have you ever thought through what makes you - you?

Are you aware of what really motivates you?

For three days, keep a running log of what you do from when you get up until when you go to bed (30-minute increments is normally sufficient). Then, analyze your days.

What are your tradeoffs?

What did you do and not do?

What did you say yes to and no to - either overtly or by default?

How does this analysis redefine your previous answers?

What are you willing to leverage? And for what?

What are you afraid of losing?

# 8

# DEFINE YOUR IMPACT
## CREATING A LEGACY

If your name is Gigoo and you are a chicken, you are living the good life – as far as chickens go. Gigoo is a rare Scots Dumpy hen. She also is the heiress of Miles Blackwell, a British publishing mogul. He left $15 million behind to Gigoo to live out her life in the Oxfordshire countryside.

I'm sure Gigoo is appreciative. Yet I wonder if that is the way you are planning to appropriate your financial legacy. For that matter, what plans do you have for leaving a legacy of any kind?

## THE PULL OF LEGACY

How do you want to be remembered? A greater issue is the lasting impact of your life. This is especially significant when you consider your life's ripple effect extends out *ad infinitum*.

When children dream of the future, they often see themselves in some heroic act: scoring a last second shot, entering a burning building to save those in distress, defeating the evil villain when everyone else cowers in fear, or being so desired by the handsome prince that he would attempt anything to save her.

Even in adulthood, desires for greatness often remain – but they may become refocused. Adults are inspired by different things.

Not everyone wants to have their name in lights or to appear on stage. Some would rather stay in the background – perhaps by making an impact from within an organization. Even so, there is a deep longing to make a difference – to leave behind something for which they will be remembered.

Does leaving a legacy sound too heady? Some will answer, "Absolutely not!" Others will manifest a bit more hesitancy. Nevertheless, you have been designed to leave one. You have that significance, that level of value.

C.S. Lewis – prolific author, amazing thinker, atheist turned theologian – looked at how genuine Christians will ultimately be glorified. They will reign in a new body, be given a new name to reflect their new existence, while fully comprehending why they were created. Based on this underlying belief he gives this challenge:

> …to remember that the dullest and most uninteresting person you talk to may one day be a creature which, if you saw it now, you would be strongly tempted to worship, or else a horror and a corruption such as you now meet, if at all, only in a nightmare…

# DEFINE YOUR IMPACT

There are no ordinary people. You have never talked to a mere mortal. Nations, cultures, arts, civilizations – these are mortal, and their life is to ours as the life of a gnat. But it is immortals whom we joke with, work with, marry, snub, and exploit – immortal horrors or everlasting splendors.[1]

Dallas Willard – an equally brilliant psychologist from the University of Southern California – quoted and then expanded upon C.S. Lewis' thoughts:

Strangely, it is precisely the intrinsic greatness of the person that makes it in its ruined condition "a horror and a corruption which as you now meet... only in a nightmare." If we were insignificant, our ruin would not be horrifying.[2]

Here's the rub: maturity often means we get a more realistic view on life. Our once lofty dreams get tempered by time. Unfortunately, many of us go from dreams of heroism and legacy to just desires for the weekend and retirement – goals we have reasonable hope of attaining. We may think, "If I make a little more money, I can change the quality of my weekends and even my sense of security about retirement."

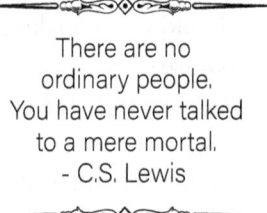

There are no ordinary people. You have never talked to a mere mortal.
- C.S. Lewis

Wherever you end up on the spectrum from visions of heroism to settling for an exciting weekend, are you attending to the ultimate value of your life?

## The Power of Legacy

Your life has extraordinary value and power. This is seen in the importance to the beliefs which inspire your life. These may have faded during all of the crises and difficulties of life – particularly those once grandiose ideas which now appear empty.

> If we were insignificant, our ruin would not be horrifying.
> - Dallas Willard

But challenges – and even failures – do not change the reality of what is true. You have innate value and potential eternal value far beyond what you can imagine.

Billy Graham wrote:

> Our days are numbered. One of the primary goals in our lives should be to prepare for the day on which your number is up. The legacy we leave is not just in our possessions, but in the quality of our lives. What preparations should we be making now? The greatest waste in all of our earth, which cannot be recycled or reclaimed, is our waste of the time God has given us each day. [3]

The power of the ripple effect of your life far exceeds the power of any individual act. An effective legacy outstrips dramatic success every time.

Put in mathematical terms, the difference in impact between Success, Significance and Soul is the same as the difference between addition, multiplication and exponentials.

Would you rather have $10 + 9$, $10 \times 9$, or $10^9$ dollars? This is the difference between $19, $90, and a billion dollars.

Previously we confronted the reality of the connection between tradeoffs and leverage. Everything is a tradeoff. When you use your tradeoffs as leverage, you open up a whole new vista for your future – for leverage is a legacy-maker.

Yet how does leverage operate in your life? You are approaching leverage in one of three ways.

## Life without Leverage

The majority live predominately without leverage or with only minimal use of it. That doesn't mean they have no impact. It merely means if they want greater impact they see one recourse – work harder.

The more advanced version of this approach is working smarter. This can include getting degrees, expanding abilities, and becoming the celebrated "Renaissance man" – cultured, knowledgeable and proficient in a wide range of fields. Of course, when greater leverage is available, it is questionable whether living life without leverage is actually smarter.

Life without leverage has the potential to expand as far as we are able to develop through our personal efforts. When we restrict ourselves in this way, we are not actually leveraging our lives, we are merely adding to them. Some do quite well with this – but it can get exhausting over time. Therefore, in many cases, the tendency is to just get by.

## Life with Horizontal Leverage

Horizontal leverage consists of leveraging to get more of the same. Financial products, the stock market, and real estate are types of horizontal leverage. You leverage the financial capital you have in order to benefit from some form of dividend, interest or appreciation.

Einstein once said, "Compound interest is the eighth wonder of the world. He who understands it, earns it. He who doesn't, pays it."

It's amazing what is possible. In a day when credit and the entrepreneurial spirit are rampant, horizontal leverage is readily available.

Mortgages are a very common forms of financial leverage. Over the past 30 years, home ownership has remained near 60%. Of those who own homes, very few could afford to pay the full price for their home. Presently with a $6,000 down payment, you can purchase a $200,000 house. In this economy you can leverage your down payment with personal credit and the appraised value of the home – allowing you to control more than 25 times your original investment.

Another common form of horizontal leverage is demonstrated when companies hire employees to multiply the capability and capacity of their business. Up to a point, the more you exploit horizontal leverage, the greater the impact you enjoy. By multiplying an existing resource you can produce increasingly more within the same general category. For example, money can be leveraged to obtain some other form of asset which has monetary value.

The payoff of this type of leverage is that it holds great value as a tool. Unfortunately, if what you had initially was an insufficient reason for being, more of the same gets you no closer to your *raison d'être*. Having more tofu doesn't change its taste.

## LIFE WITH VERTICAL LEVERAGE

Vertical leverage, however, produces outcomes which are fundamentally different.

The concept of having a forward-looking vision is nothing new. You probably have read or heard numerous challenges about the importance of clarifying vision.

In 1980 Bill Gates envisioned, "a computer on every desk and in every home" – a lofty idea for that day. In 1962 John F. Kennedy believed we would put a man on the moon by the end of the decade – another rather lofty idea – but one we accomplished by the end of July 1969. We've previously referred to Martin Luther King, Jr. and Sir Winston Churchill. These were impactful people because their visions extended far beyond themselves.

In his, *Start with Why*, Simon Sinek surmised that, "The goal is not to give you a course of action. The goal is to offer you the cause of action." Sinek proposed a unique level of motivation – a "Why" that changed one's impact from merely achieving more to truly achieving something different.

He distinguishes his "Why" this way:

> In the business world, they say Apple is a lifestyle brand. They underestimate Apple's power. Gucci is a lifestyle brand – Apple changes the course of industries. By any definition these few companies don't function like corporate entities. They exist as social movements. [4]

Vertical leverage is built on a vision beyond ourselves of something far greater than what we can accomplish on our own – something exponentially greater than what we originally leveraged.

Jim Elliot had this kind of vision. He grew up with a passion to make a difference for people who didn't have the opportunities he had. He was saddened by people living their lives without knowing the God he knew.

Jim had grown up in Portland, Oregon; the people of Quito, Ecuador were over 4,000 miles away. In the early 1950's it took 18 days by ship to get to Ecuador. But Jim had a passion, a sense of calling, to make a difference there. In 1952 the 25-year-old set out to reach the Ecuadorian Huaorani tribe often known as the Auca Indians. "Auca" was the word for "savage."

Jim Elliot and his four missionary friends had spent months contacting the Auca tribe from the safety of a small plane. They had designed a system by which they could give gifts, trade, and communicate friendship without ever having to land their plane. At that time no one, even from that area, would dare try to interact face to face with the Aucas.

Out of a desire to help the tribe, they had spent months befriending them. Finally, the team landed on a sandbar near a couple of the Auca villages.

> During a supply flight, Saint [the team's pilot] spotted a large party of Aucas approaching. He quickly landed, and the missionaries prepared to greet their visitors. The Aucas attacked. They skewered the Christians with spears and hacked [them] down with stolen machetes. In a frenzy they peeled the fabric from the fuselage of the plane and twisted its steel landing struts.[5]

Life Magazine later sent their photographer, Cornell Capa, to chronical the story. In Cornell's words the Auca tribe was made up of "the worst people on earth." Based on local reports, he wrote:

> Murder was the most significant cause of death among the Aucas. Seventy-four per cent of all Auca men died through violent tribal warfare. When one of their number got sick or old, his relatives dug a pit beneath his hammock, toppled him in, and buried him alive. The tribe suffered a shortage of women because mothers often strangled girl babies with a vine as soon as they were born. One Auca mother of twins said, "I was so frightened to see two babies appear, instead of just one, that I buried them." The Aucas killed for sport, lust, jealousy or out of simple irritation. One Indian speared both his friend's wife and mother to death as a joke.[6]

The tribe had lived up to their Auca name. It cost Jim Elliot and his four missionary friends their lives. The attack left Elisabeth, Jim's wife of two-and-a-half years, as a widow, and Valerie, his eleven-month-old daughter, fatherless.

Three years prior, as a senior in college, Jim had revealed the vertical leverage that motivated him to put his life at risk. In his private journal he penned these immortal words, "He is no fool who gives what he cannot keep to gain that which he cannot lose."

Amazingly his wife, daughter, and the families of the others slain in the attack went back to the same villages, befriended the people, showed them love and forgiveness, and won over the entire tribe both as friends and ultimately as Christian believers.

A spokesman from Mission Aviation Fellowship related this many years later:

> In the years since Saint [Elliot's pilot] and his fellows were killed, quite a few Christians – I would estimate several thousand in the overall missionary community – have dedicated their own lives to Christ because of the example of these men. [Missionary Aviation Fellowship] constantly gets applications from people who have been inspired by the story. This is still going on right now.[7]

According to research done by James Boster, professor of anthropology at the University of Connecticut, the conversion and transformation of the Waorani people (called "Auca") brought them from the "point of extinction," due to their internal violence, to a peaceful and successful tribe.[8] Their tribe eventually expanded to four times its previous size.

Not only had Jim and his team's life-leverage resulted in the entire tribe being transformed, it also ignited a generation of people committed to giving themselves for the benefit of others. Over 50 years later cultures are still being transformed by people initially inspired because of Jim Elliot and his teammates' investment of their lives.

This is the exponential effect of vertical leverage.

## Degrees of Impact

The quality of life of someone living from the Soul level

drastically exceeds living with Success as the bottom line. In fact, maturing beyond a mere pursuit of Success to a life motivated by Soul is valuable for a far greater reason than that "it makes me feel more fulfilled"— even though that is true. This transformation is truly an inspired life – a life lived out of the essential devotion to something or someone greater than yourself.

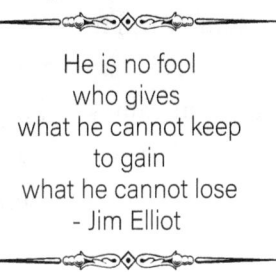

Success, Significance and Soul all have value and are focused on making impact. It is especially in the impact of each of these that their true extent and worth is revealed.

The draw and the benefit of Success is that it is both readily quantifiable and creates the most immediate impact. For example: you complete a job; it creates a product; it results in income and benefit to an individual or community.

Further, a distinguishing mark of Success is that it is expendable. It is an asset or product that is used up or may even have limited shelf life. Even though the Success itself may take time to create, its impact is often relatively immediate and temporary.

Significance, on the hand, always takes time to fully develop. Universally it has a prolonged incubation period while it builds an expanding benefit. Protégés are mentored; business cultures are changed; communities are revitalized. The impact of Significance is most clearly seen in the altering of the course of lives.

If the impact of Success is seen as being comparatively immediate, Significance's impact would be described as much more extended.

Success can be achieved without reference to other people. We may incorporate people in its development. But when I quantify it, I'm not referring to how people are benefited or hindered. Success may be used to impact others, but we are specifically speaking of the visible, measureable effects of a job done exceptionally well.

Significance *requires* impact on others. Therefore, Significance can carry on long beyond the lifetime of its originator through the people it impacts. While any impact can fade with time, conversely it also can build organically. The extended effects of Significance separate it from the far more transient impact of Success.

The impact of Soul, however, is the pinnacle of human influence and achievement. Soul speaks to the most intimately personal level of purpose – a heart cry, a sense of calling, a *raison d'être*. Because you weren't thoughtlessly created, the Soul level has a profound impact when it is well executed.

Regardless of your specific beliefs about God, there is an inherent understanding that something infinitely greater than ourselves is behind what exists and especially why it exists.

*As you step into business, if you assume you must cover up or restrain your most deeply held beliefs – your Soul level – you are cutting off your greatest source of impact.*

You have been uniquely designed to make an impact. When your Significance and the way you approach Success most precisely coincides with that design, the extent of your impact becomes eternal. The word eternal has religious overtones, but I'm speaking as much to the quality of your impact as I am the quantity in years.

Everything about living out of the Soul level builds toward a greater impact. When you are in sync with your design, even difficulties are more palatable. When you are out of sync, even Success feels distasteful. Even though you may see only a fraction of the ultimate effect, the instinctive awareness that you are "on to something" becomes prevalent and empowering.

There is a fundamental quality difference to a Soul-level impact. It is very much like your soul lives on in the impact it has created. In business we don't usually speak in such terms, but as a consequence we struggle to understand how to replicate the leadership and culture of those who have lived out of the Soul level.

## Cost

To experience Soul requires a maximum investment. It involves more than one's time. It requires internal leverage, risking everything.

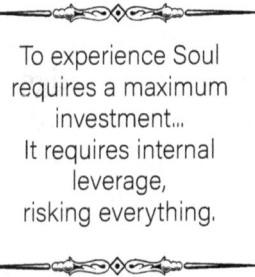

To experience Soul requires a maximum investment... It requires internal leverage, risking everything.

At the Success level, investing can be done at an emotional distance. Although investing at the Significance level requires an emotional connection, Soul requires your heart. It involves both the power and the pain of a complete risk in order to achieve your true calling.

The desire to impress others, to live with ease, to live with an existential benefit pulls us away from Soul. Living out of Soul is the exact opposite of the existential approach to life. If "existence precedes essence" – as the existentialist believes – then I must create my own meaning. But if I have been designed, I have the restful opportunity to live in harmony with that design.

We clearly recognize that a screwdriver has a specific functional design. Yet if a screwdriver believed it had to figure out its own reason for being, it would face an immense probability of getting it wrong.

Similarly, failing to live out of the Soul level inevitably leads to a tragically unfulfilled life.

On the other hand, it is an "all-in" risk to put the eggs of my reason for being into the one basket of Soul. A life lived "all-in" at the Soul level means dying to every other source of value.

There are several reasons why fully living out of Soul requires risking my Success and Significance in order to do so. Fundamentally, that risk is necessary because, by living out of Soul, I have chosen to accept the Soul level as the truest part of who I am.

You don't have to be a philosopher to grasp this. Simply put, you were designed – you are meant to be something. Risk everything to discover your meaning and to live it out.

The ultimate purveyor of Soul, Jesus, illuminated the real bottom line:

> For whoever wishes to save his life will lose it; but whoever loses his life for My sake will find it. For what will it

profit a man if he gains the whole world and forfeits his soul? Or what will a man give in exchange for his soul?[9]

There is intense competition between the attraction of the intrinsic value we sense within ourselves versus a similarly powerful desire to survive. Oddly enough, to deny myself is not to reject myself. Instead, it is to live beyond the control of my basest emotions so that I can enjoy my most fundamental meaning: my inherently designed purpose.

If I gain everything but lose the reason I exist, what good is it?

## Beyond Crafting a Vision

In 1954 Peter Drucker described the leadership approach of management by objectives (MBO) – a means of leading through objectives mutually agreed upon between management and employees.

More recently Roberto Verganti suggested the reason why innovators like Steve Jobs were so successful is they have discovered a new approach to leading a company: management by meaning (MBM). MBM is focused on the creation of meaning for both customers and employees.

These two approaches need not be mutually exclusive. In fact, they both refer to leadership that progressively moves deeper and deeper into the heart of those being led. Therefore, they both ultimately result in the culture being impacted. These leadership processes move beyond attempting to affect action – progressively harnessing and transforming thinking into a better reflection of the leaders and his employees' Soul.

MBO doesn't just tell employees what to do. It involves them in clarifying the goals and objectives, then shares the rewards when the objectives are reached. This naturally creates a motivation beyond dictated orders, or monetary carrots, by creating a greater sense of involvement and fulfillment.

MBM takes it one step further. The motivating idea – that what you are developing has meaning – becomes fundamental to what you do when you show up to work. It starts long before creating strategies to get a job done. It begins by asking how do we create meaning through what we design and produce.

For instance, TOMS created meaning out of the simple business of designing shoes. On its website, TOMS declares its motivating principle – "Every purchase has a purpose. Through your purchase, TOMS helps provide shoes, sight and water to people in need." TOMS has gradually expanded what they produce beyond just shoes to eyewear, coffee, and bags. This is how they describe the start of the process of product development: "Launching a new One for One giving product always starts with identifying a need."

If your life approach is taken from Larry the Cable Guy, then your next thought is let's "git 'er done." Let's craft a vision, decide on a plan, and begin executing. I confess "a moth to the flame" attraction to anyone who has that can-do and will-do attitude toward life. I believe it is significantly more productive than the tendency to spend enormous eras of life philosophizing or introspectively analyzing the potential future.

"Do something already!" is more valuable than

philosophizing. The challenge with this attitude, however, is that it spins us right back into the "action crisis" we addressed at the beginning of the book: a frustration with pursuing actions that just keep boomeranging back to where you started – or merely stall out.

If your "vision" is just "a bright shiny object" which recently caught your attention – or the result of an emotionally-inspiring event – when the pressure inevitably hits, your motivation will wither.

Neither is the true meaning of MBM achieved by picking something out of the air. A connection at the Soul level is needed – not just crafting a vision, but discovering one.

In his classic tale, Goethe had Faust say,

> You can't, if you can't feel it, if it never
> > Rises from the soul, and sways
> > The heart of every single hearer,
> > With deepest power, in simple ways.
> > You'll sit forever, gluing things together,
> > Cooking up a stew from other's scraps,
> > Blowing on a miserable fire,
> > Made from your heap of dying ash.
> > Let apes and children praise your art,
> > If their admiration's to your taste,
> > But you'll never speak from heart to heart,
> > Unless it rises up from your heart's space.[10]

We desire admiration. We also have an intense instinct and desire for self-preservation.

To the degree that Goldstein and then Maslow got it

right, my ability to pursue "self-actualization" is dependent on how successfully I have achieved my internal desire for physiological, safety, love, belonging, and esteem needs.

Yet "self-actualization" doesn't avoid the potential rollercoaster of fear or lack that periodically bubbles up from the baser levels of my needs. The desperate desire to meet these basic needs causes our life to be lived in the spin cycle. Is there a way to not merely avoid the spin cycle but actually turn it off?

I can only meet this need when I learn to live at the Soul level.

## Pause

In order to broaden your impact, you also must learn to pause.

Legacies don't happen by accident. There is a natural static that drowns out, or at least obscures, an otherwise clear understanding of purpose.

Charles Hummel wrote in his book, *Tyranny of the Urgent*:

> Your greatest danger is letting the urgent things crowd out the important.
> There is an insidious tendency to neglect important tasks that do not have to be done today – or even this week.[11]

Your primary task is to understand the reason you are here. This task is only exceeded by the need to know the

# DEFINE YOUR IMPACT

One who created the reason you are here.

If you are content to live "paycheck-to-paycheck" – not only in your bank account but also in your soul – then ignore the necessity to pause. But if you wish to build a legacy, then reject the pressure to run without retreat.

There is an enormous tendency to presume, to the point of belief, that life involves what you always thought it involved. We believe our gut-level assumptions are reality. When pursuing what we think is best, our natural instincts are to just modify the way we are already living. But those who have created a legacy discover the greatest effect is found in a lifestyle of purposeful, focused pausing.

The life which Jesus exemplified went way beyond a moralistic parable. His life defined more than the best way to live. It was the true way to live.

Jesus not only had the humanly impossible task of being the Savior. He also had the challenge of communicating to people who had a highly distorted idea of what being the Messiah meant and what God intended for any area of life.

On top of that, he had religious leaders, who were apoplectically fanatical about stopping him, tripping him up, or just creating havoc about him. If you've ever tried to do something incredibly difficult while a group of powerful people made a concerted effort to screw up your plan – then you get the point. Today's political turmoil looks like child's play in comparison.

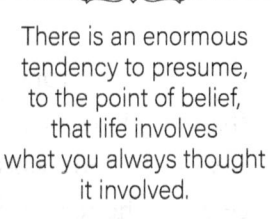

There is an enormous tendency to presume, to the point of belief, that life involves what you always thought it involved.

These brilliant, educated, cultural leaders did everything they could to undermine Jesus' impact and legacy.

Here's how it went down and how Jesus responded to this insanity:

> Finally the temple guards went back to the chief priests and the Pharisees, who asked them, "Why didn't you bring him in?" "No one ever spoke the way this man does," the guards replied. "You mean he has deceived you also?" the Pharisees retorted. "Have any of the rulers or of the Pharisees believed in him? No! But this mob that knows nothing of the law—there is a curse on them." Nicodemus, who had gone to Jesus earlier and who was one of their own number, asked, "Does our law condemn a man without first hearing him to find out what he has been doing?" They replied, "Are you from Galilee, too? Look into it, and you will find that a prophet does not come out of Galilee." Then they all went home,
>
> But Jesus went to the Mount of Olives. At dawn he appeared again in the temple courts, where all the people gathered around him, and he sat down to teach them.[12]

Get this: everyone else just went home and binged on Netflix, or whatever they did in the first century AD, and then went to bed. Jesus went to the Mount of Olives, the place where he repeatedly got away.

Again and again after significant times of impact, he would get away to pause. For him that meant communicating with his heavenly Father.

Jesus constantly was getting clarity. The pressure on

him was immense. No one fully understood his intent, even though it wasn't for any lack of him communicating to them. Under the circumstances, our tendency would be to just crash. His was to pause.

As a result, Jesus was back at it in the morning, unswayed and unpanicked – instead, focused and clear.

Live like he lived.

My challenge to you: don't just do something. Don't just do something that is good. In fact, don't just do something that is good, excellent, valuable, and needed.

Instead, do something that is all of those qualities but is also what you have been created to do – which may require you to first pause in order to find out what that is.

Anything less will not only be unfulfilling but will blunt your ultimate impact.

Living life from a place of meaning – which is living from the level of Soul – has amazing power and impact

But real Soul-pursuit will cost you. Its most tangible cost is the willingness to release the more superficial motivators of Success and Significance – to risk them and leverage them in accomplishing something much greater.

The call is to a commitment to let go of the desperate desire for self-preservation. When you discover that you don't have to survive, it frees you. Live beyond a need for personal Success.

To leave a legacy – indeed, to live a legacy – requires a belief, a trust, in something greater than yourself. You have only so much focus, only so much understanding. This means you have a very limited source of trust and life to expend.

To live at the highest level, your ultimate trust must rest

on one final Source. Your Success and Significance must bow before that Source. But if you give Success, Significance, and Soul equal billing, they will wipe out the power of living from the Soul level.

Discover this secret of living, and you will experience the full *Power of Belief in Business*.

# BELIEF TRANSFORMATION

## Chapter 8
Calibrate your beliefs:

- Your life's ripple effect extends out ad infinitum.

- There are no ordinary people. If we were insignificant, our ruin would not be horrifying.

- You have innate value and potential eternal value far beyond what you can imagine.

- An effective legacy outstrips dramatic success every time.

- Leverage is a legacy-maker.

- Life without leverage – great impact comes by working harder or even working smarter – but only if working smarter refers to greater learning.

- Live with horizontal leverage – leveraging to get more of the same – e.g., compound interest, mortgages, expanded employee base.

- Life with vertical leverage – produces outcomes which are fundamentally different from what was leveraged – e.g., actions that transform cultures, lives that influence future generations, endeavors that change the quality of life and eternity.

- Living at the Soul level is achieved by people living out of the essential devotion to something or someone greater than themselves.

- *Success* is readily quantifiable, makes immediate impact, and is expendable.

- *Significance* always takes time to develop; its impact is more extended and requires impact on others.

- *Soul* is the pinnacle of human influence and achievement, is the most intimately personal of all pursuits, and connects with something infinitely greater than the person themselves.

- As you step into business, if you believe you must cover up or restrain your most deeply held beliefs – your Soul level – you are cutting off your greatest source of impact.

- Soul requires maximum investment and cannot be done at an emotional distance.

- If I gain everything but lose the reason I exist, what good is it?

- Management by meaning (MBM) is a powerful way to lead, but impactful meaning isn't something that can just be plucked out of the air.

- If you wish to build a legacy, then reject the pressure to run without retreat.

- There is an enormous tendency to presume, to the point of belief, that life involves what you always thought it involved.

## DEFINE YOUR IMPACT

- Do what you have been created to do!
- Live beyond a need for personal success.

How do you define your personal value?

How leveraged is your life?

Is there a Soul legacy you desire to leave? How would you define it?

Are you passionate enough for some Soul calling that you would risk your Success, even your Significance, to achieve it?

Where are you tempted to pursue immediate impact or results even though it will limit or undermine your ultimate chance to experience a legacy?

# NOTES

## Introduction

1 Verganti, R. (2014, July 23). Steve Jobs and Management by Meaning. Harvard Business Review. https://hbr.org/2011/10/steve-jobs-and-management-by-m
2 "Civilization," Ralph Waldo Emerson

## Chapter 1

1 Beetz, K. (n.d.). Lay, Ken 1942– | Encyclopedia.com. Encyclopedia.Com. Retrieved October 18, 2017, from https://www.encyclopedia.com/economics/news-wires-white-papers-and-books/lay-ken-1942
2 Hurt, H., III. (1996, August 5). "Power Players." Fortune, 134(3), 94-97. Online archive https://archive.fortune.com/magazines/fortune/fortune_archive/1996/08/05/215462/index.htm

3   Stein, N. (2000, October 2). "The World's Most Admired Companies." Fortune, 142(7), 182-190.
4   Novak, M. (1996). Business as a Calling: Work and the Examined Life (First edition, first printing (full number line) ed.). Free Press.
5   Beetz, K. (n.d.). Lay, Ken 1942– | Encyclopedia.com. Encyclopedia.Com. Retrieved October 18, 2017, from https://www.encyclopedia.com/economics/news-wires-white-papers-and-books/lay-ken-1942
6   Sunseri, G., & Rottman, S. (2006, May 25). Enron Verdict: Ken Lay Guilty on All Counts, Skilling on 19 Counts. Retrieved October 18, 2017, from http://abcnews.go.com/Business/LegalCenter/story?id=2003728&page=1
7   U.S.Cong., Committee on Energy and Commerce. (n.d.). "Oath Taking, Truth Telling, and Remedies in the Business World" [Cong. Rept. 107-121 from 107th Cong., 2nd sess.].
8   "Apollo Robbins, The Master Pickpocket Tricks of the Trade." YouTube. Viral.Tosh, 09 Nov. 2013. Web. 26 Nov. 2013.
9   NationalGeographic. "Apollo Robbins on Lying | Brain Games." YouTube. YouTube, 18 June 2013. Web. 20 Apr. 2017.
10  Voss. C. (2016). *Never Split the Difference – Negotiating As If Your Life Depended On It.* London: Random House Business Books, 5-8.
11  Ibid, 12, 84.

## Chapter 2

1. Kennedy, Dane. "Forgotten Failures of African Exploration." The Public Domain Review. N.p., 22 Apr. 2015. Web. 22 Feb. 2017.
2. Tuckey, Captain J.K., R.N. (1818). *Narrative of an Expedition to Explore the River Zaire, Usually Called the Congo, in South Africa, in 1816*. London: John Murray.
3. Kennedy, Dane. "Forgotten Failures of African Exploration." The Public Domain Review. N.p., 22 Apr. 2015. Web. 22 Feb. 2017.
4. Golding, V. (2013, orig. 1906). The Story of David Livingstone (Illustrated). Didactic Press, 1.
5. Ibid, 48,66.

## Chapter 3

1. "cheat". Dictionary.com Unabridged. Random House, Inc. 3 May. 2017. <Dictionary.com http://www.dictionary.com/browse/cheat>.
2. Bishop, Michael, Chair of the Iowa State University Department of Philosophy and Religion. "What's Wrong with Cheating?" quoted by the Dean of Students - California State Univ. San Marcos, n.d. Web. 03 May 2017.
3. Cohen, Herb (2003). *Negotiate This! By Caring But Not T-H-A-T Much.* New York, NY.: Warner, 27-28.

## Chapter 4

1. Taylor, Richard Shelley (1962). *The disciplined life*. Kansas City, MO: Beacon Hill Press, 29.

## Chapter 5

1. apply. (n.d.). Dictionary.com Unabridged. Retrieved July 1, 2017 from Dictionary.com website http://www.dictionary.com/browse/apply
2. Bennis, W. G., & Nanus, B. (1995). *Leaders: the strategies for taking charge*. Oxford, San Francisco: Jossey-Bass Publ, 25.
3. Counterintuitive. (n.d.). Retrieved August 22, 2017, from http://www.oxfordreference.com/search?q=counterintuitive&searchBtn=Search&isQuickSearch=true
4. Turner, D. A. (2015). *Its My Pleasure: The Impact of Extraordinary Talent and a Compelling Culture*. Boise: Elevate, 70, 118.
5. Ibid, 120.
6. Interview, South Africa, 1986 (Part I). http://logotherapy.univie.ac.at/e/clipgallery.html

## Chapter 6

1. George B. (2015). *Discover Your True North*. Hoboken, NJ: Wiley, 109.
2. Ibid, 110.
3. Sinek, S. (2011). *Start With Why: How Great Leaders Inspire Everyone to Take Action*. London: Portfolio Penguin, 38.
4. Ibid, 2.
5. The terms Success, Significance and Soul are capitalized throughout when referring to levels of purpose so as to distinguish the titles from the general use of the same terms.

6. Buford, B. (1994). *Half Time: Changing Your Game Plan From Success to Significance*. Grand Rapids, MI: Zondervan, 25.
7. Sinek, S. (2011). *Start With Why: How Great Leaders Inspire Everyone to Take Action*. London: Portfolio Penguin, 134.
8. job. (n.d.). Dictionary.com Unabridged. Retrieved December 12, 2017 from Dictionary.com website http://www.dictionary.com/browse/job

## CHAPTER 7

1. Shaw, G. B. (2004). *Man and Superman*. 1st World Library Literacy Society, 37.
2. Bradberry, T. (2015, January 20). "Multitasking Damages Your Brain And Career, New Studies Suggest." Retrieved December 29, 2017, from https://www.forbes.com/sites/travisbradberry/2014/10/08/multitasking-damages-your-brain-and-career-new-studies-suggest/#-4614f44756ee
3. Gorlick, A. (2016, April 15). "Media multitaskers pay mental price, Stanford study shows." Retrieved December 29, 2017, from https://news.stanford.edu/2009/08/24/multitask-research-study-082409/
4. Maxwell, J. C. (1998). *The 21 Irrefutable Laws of Leadership: Follow Them and People Will Follow You*. Nashville, TN: Thomas Nelson, 189.

## Chapter 8

1. Willard, D. (2012). *Renovation of the Heart: Putting On the Character of Christ.* Colorado Springs, CO: NavPress, 45, 46.
2. Ibid, 46.
3. Graham, B. (2011). *Hope For a Troubled Heart: Finding God In the Midst of Pain.* Thomas Nelson.
4. Sinek, S. (2011). *Start With Why: How Great Leaders Inspire Everyone to Take Action.* London: Portfolio Penguin, 148.
5. Cowart, J. W. (n.d.). "The Worst People on Earth." Retrieved March 19, 2018, from http://www.cowart.info/AucasTheWorstPeopleOnEarth.htm
6. Ibid.
7. Ibid.
8. "Anthropologist studies tribe noted for missionary killings." (2016, January 30). http://advance.uconn.edu/2006/060130/06013008.htm
9. Matthew 16:25, 26 New American Standard Bible
10. Johann Wolfgang von Goethe, *Faust: First Part*
11. Hummel, C. (1967). *Tyranny of the Urgent.* Downers Grove, IL: IVP Books, 5, 22.
12. John 7:45-8:2 New International Version

www.ingramcontent.com/pod-product-compliance
Lightning Source LLC
Chambersburg PA
CBHW051828160426
43209CB00040B/1982/J